Amazon Echo Auto

The Complete User Guide:
Learn to Use Your Echo Auto Like A Pro

by C.J. Andersen

Copyright © 2019 by CJ Andersen — All rights reserved.

AMAZON ECHO AUTO is a trademark of Amazon Technologies Inc. All other copyrights & trademarks are the properties of their respective owners. Reproduction of any part of this book without the permission of the copyright owners is illegal — the only exception to this is the inclusion of brief quotes in a review of the work. Any request for permission should be directed to cjandersentech@gmail.com

Contents

Introduction

Before the We Get Started: Echo Auto Basics   **8**

What is Echo Auto and Does it Work?   9
The Echo Auto Preview   10
Specifications of the Amazon Echo Auto   11

1: Let's Begin! – Echo Auto Setup   **13**

Downloading the Alexa App   13
Connecting Echo Auto to your Car   14
Connecting Echo Auto to the Alexa App   13
Troubleshooting Echo Auto Setup   13
Troubleshooting Echo Auto Bluetooth Connection   15
Add another Alexa-enabled device to your Echo Auto   16
Creating Your Voice Profile   16
Creating an Amazon Household   17

2: Meet the Alexa App   **19**

The App and Your Voice   19
The Alexa App Homepage   20

3: The 'Now Playing' Page and Player   **23**

4: Songs by the Millions — Music   **26**

My Music Library/ My Amazon Music   27
Amazon Prime Music   30
Add Prime Playlists to My Music Library   33
Spotify   34
Pandora   36
iHeartRadio   38
TuneIn   40
SiriusXM   42
Deezer   44
Other Music/ Radio Skills   44
Setting Default Music Service   44

5: Tell Me a Story – Books   **46**

Audible   46

Kindle Books	48

6: Write it Down & Get it Done — Lists   **50**

Shopping Lists	51
To-do Lists	52
Create Your Own List	53
Delete a List	53

7: Never Forget, Always Be On Time   **55**
— Reminders, Alarms & Timers

Reminders	55
Alarms	57
Timers	59

8: Let's See What She Can Do — Alexa Skills   **60**

Get Familiar with Skills	60
Enable Skills and Use Them	64
Disable a Skill	65
Alexa Skills Blueprint	66

9: 21st Century Living — Smart Home   **67**

Set Up Smart Home Devices via Skills	68
Set Up Groups, Scenes and Routines	70
Troubleshooting Alexa and Smart Home Device Set Up	74

10: Your Highly Capable Personal Assistant   **75**
— Things to Try

What's New?	76
Ask Questions	77
Check and Manage Your Calendar	77
Discover New Alexa Skills	77
Find Local Businesses and Restaurants	78
Find Traffic Information	79
Get Weather Forecasts	79
Go to the Movies	80
Hear the News – Flash Briefing	80
Get Your Sports Updates	81
Calling and Messaging	82
Drop In	84
Announcements	85
Kids and Safety	86

11: Perfect Fit – Alexa Settings   87

Your Profile   87
Voice Purchasing   87
Amazon Household Profile   87
Deleting Voice Recordings   87
Device Settings   88
Your Locations   88
Privacy and Permissions Management   88
Choose Default Music Services   88
Flash Briefing   88
Traffic, Sports, Calendars and Lists   89

12: Resources Galore — Help & Feedback   91

13. Going to the Source – Amazon Pages to Be Familiar With   94

Before You Go   95

Introduction

Hello and welcome! Thank you for buying this Amazon Echo Auto user guide and I look forward to sharing my knowledge and helping you to master your new Amazon device. Before we get under way I would like to make a couple of suggestions. Firstly, I would like to encourage you to get familiar with Amazon's Help Pages and here's why... Amazon is constantly tweaking, updating and expanding the capabilities of both its devices (Fire tablets, Fire TV, Echo, Echo Auto, Echo Dot, Echo Show etc) and its AI software Alexa.

And when I say constantly, I mean ALL the time.

While I will continue to publish updated editions of this guide, I want to be sure that anyone who has bought this book has the chance to stay up to date with the frequent changes and Amazon's help pages for your device is the best place to do that. When changes to the way your device works or new features are introduced, the information is also updated on these help pages. Personally, I don't find their help pages super user-friendly, but nevertheless they are the best place to stay up to date with changes and improvements.

Secondly, I wanted to say a word about this guide, how it has been put together and the best way to use it. Of course, you should feel free to go straight to a particular chapter if there is some specific information you are looking for, but I would also urge you to read the book in its entirety as it follows a logical progression.

I have laid out this guide in a logical, step by step sequence; from setting up your Echo Auto through explaining every menu page within the Alexa App, starting at the top and working down to the bottom. It's really the easiest way to approach and master Alexa without jumping back and forth and getting lost in the numerous options.

I'll also be reviewing the many third-party apps and Alexa Skills that you can access via the Echo Auto to maximize your enjoyment of the device, including:

— Using music apps such as Amazon Music, Spotify, TuneIn and iHeartRadio

— Linking up to audiobook services like Audible and Kindle

— Controlling Smart Home technology via the Echo Auto

— Getting the most out of the Alexa personal assistant, from hand-free calling to getting directions!

— And, of course, troubleshooting common glitches that crop up from time to time...

I am confident that anyone, no matter what level their tech skills, will find learning and using their Amazon Echo Auto pretty straightforward. If there's anything that you still find confusing after having read this guide then please email me at cjandersentech@gmail.com

Okay, let's go!

Before We Get Started: Echo Auto Basics

I was an enthusiastic early-adopter of the original Amazon Echo, and was very happy with its performance from the start; so much so that I went on to invest in several other Echo devices to use in different locations in my home which I use all the time to:

- Set alarms and daily reminders
- Hear the weather forecast
- Listen to music
- Get news flash briefings and traffic reports
- Speak to my other Alexa-using friends and family hands-free
- Control my smart home devices

I particularly appreciate that most of the information requested from Echo also shows up on the Alexa App (more later), so I can view it there immediately or later when I want to review it.

So, when I heard that Amazon were launching an Echo device that I could use in my car, I was very keen to get my hands on one and be able to access all those great Alexa features on the road!

What is Echo Auto and Does it Work?

If you've already got an Echo device at home, you'll probably have a fair idea what the Echo Auto is, but you might not be quite right in all your assumptions. And for those of you who are new to the Echo universe, here's the deal:

The Echo Auto is effectively a very, very good microphone that works in conjunction with the Alexa App on your mobile phone and with your car's stereo system, allowing you to use your voice to activate all the numerous features that Alexa offers. To be clear, the Echo Auto on its own will not work – it has to be paired with the Alexa App downloaded on your phone, so that Alexa can hear your commands. And it also has to be connected to your car's stereo system, where you will then hear Alexa's replies, music etc.

The reason you'd want this product is that currently, if you have Alexa on your phone you need to press the Alexa logo in order for your phone to hear your request. Clearly, that is not at all convenient when you're driving. So, the Echo Auto will basically allow you to use Alexa hands-free in your car.

And does it work?

Yes, most of the time! There are several features that I really like about the Echo Auto: it is great for listening to music; and for making calls to my other Alexa using friends and family. I also found it was useful for asking Alexa to do tasks related to my smart home devices that were already linked into my Alexa app (like having the porch lights turn on before arriving home), for playing silly games with my kids and for adding notes to my calendar.

What I didn't like so much about Echo Auto was that the Bluetooth connection sometimes bugged out, which was annoying (see more about troubleshooting this problem in the next chapter).

The other – quite important – thing to note is that Alexa/ Amazon do not have their own navigation system. This means that if you ask Alexa for directions to a place, what she will do is link through to your phone's default navigation system, which you can then follow on your phone's screen. Whether or not Alexa also reads out the turn-by-turn directions seems to be a bit hit-and-miss depending on your phone's navigation app (Waze, Google or Apple maps seem to work fine).

However, you will definitely need a good data plan on your phone for these navigation apps to work well.

In the next chapters I will walk through exactly how to set up the Echo Auto and Alexa App so that you can get the most use of it whilst in your car.

A quick note on the wake word: Echo Auto requires a wake word to activate. For example, "Alexa, what's the weather like today" where "Alexa" is your wake word. I'm guessing you already know that, so in this guide I don't include a wake word when suggesting what to say to Alexa. For any voice command you read in this guide be sure to use your wake word first.

The Echo Auto Preview

Getting started with Echo Auto takes just a few minutes, and most of the setup happens automatically. Before you connect it, though, look over your new Echo Auto to familiarize yourself with the physical features of the hardware and the purpose of each.

The Echo Auto is a slim rectangular device, barely bigger than a pack of playing cards. There are two buttons on the top of the device:

Action Button: this is the button with the single dot; you can use it to activate Alexa without using the wake word, turn off timers and alarms.

Mic Off Button: this is the button with the image of a circle with a line drawn through it. Press and quickly release this button to turn off the microphones so that Alexa won't "hear" the wake word.

Light bar: The LED light bar goes along the front edge of the Echo Auto and gives a variety of indications:

- **Blue pulsing right to left:** Echo Auto is starting up after being plugged in.

- **Blue pulsing left/ right to center:** Alexa is processing your request/ giving you an answer.

- **Blue pulsing side to side:** Echo Auto is waiting for a Bluetooth connection.

- **Red:** The microphones have been turned off.

- **Orange side to side:** Echo Auto is ready for setup.

- **Orange pulsing:** A factory reset is in progress.

- **Purple:** Setup failed.

Power supply and port: There is a Micro-power port on the right hand side of the device.

Audio port: There is a 3.5mm audio port next to the power port.

Specifications of the Amazon Echo Auto

In case you're wondering, here are the specs of the device in front of you.

Dimensions and Weight: Size: 3.3" x 1.9" x 0.5" / 1.6 ounces

Available finishes: Black

Microphones: 8-mic array

Networking: Echo Auto connects to most cars that support Bluetooth to play music or that have an auxiliary input.

Warranty: 1 year

Note on the Echo Auto functionality

To power the Echo Auto you will either be plugging it into the cigarette lighter port (what Amazon refers to as the In-Car port) or into a USB port that is integrated to your stereo system. All the cables you need to do this are provided with the Echo Auto.

Further, as mentioned above, Echo Auto connects both to your car's stereo system via Bluetooth or auxiliary cable so make sure to check that your car's stereo has Bluetooth (version 4.0 or higher) or an integrated Auxiliary cable in port.

Finally, Echo Auto also connects to your mobile phone via the Alexa App. So, Echo Auto uses your existing smartphone plan for connectivity and carrier charges may apply. Echo Auto supports Android 6.0 and iOS 12 or greater; but Echo Auto is not currently supported on all phones. Check out this list on the Amazon website for more details: https://amzn.to/2NHfuYz

Note on the air vent mount

The Echo Auto is also supplied with a mount that attaches to your air vent; not all car air vents are compatible. You can check this here: http://bit.ly/33ia64R

1: Let's Begin!
— Echo Auto Setup

For any voice command you read in this chapter be sure to use your wake word ("Alexa", "Amazon", etc) first.

Setting up the Echo Auto is largely an automated process. Here's what should have come in the box:

- Echo Auto

- In-Car Power adapter (power adapter for your car's cigarette lighter)

- Micro USB cable (1m)

- 3.5m auxiliary cable (1m)

- Air vent mount

- Echo Auto Quick Start guide

OK, enough with the preliminaries. Let's get the Echo Auto started.

Download the Alexa App to your phone

Mobile device requirements are:

- FireOS 3.0 or higher

- Android 5.0 or higher

- iOS 9.0 or higher

The quickest method for downloading the app is to go to the app store on your mobile device, look up the Alexa App and install it.

Once the Alexa App is installed, you will be able to access it on your mobile device and at alexa.amazon.com on your PC or Mac.

Connect Echo Auto to your Car

Plug the Micro USB cable either into your car's USB port or the cigarette lighter using the adaptor supplied and (if you're using the mount) attach the mount to an air vent, with the Echo Auto light bar facing forward.

Then set your car stereo to Bluetooth. If your car stereo doesn't support Bluetooth music streaming, you can connect the Echo Auto to the auxiliary in-port using the auxiliary cable supplied. In this case, make sure your car stereo is set to AUX.

Connect your Echo Auto to the Alexa App

Access the Alexa App on your mobile phone; at the bottom of the homepage you'll see the Devices icon (a house with two switches), tap on here and then:

- Tap the + *sign* at the top of the ***Devices*** page.

- Next choose ***Add Device***.

- Choose ***Amazon Echo*** and then ***Echo Auto*** then follow the prompts on the App to finish setup.

Note that the Alexa App may ask you to accept some permissions, such as accessing your location and microphone – these are essential for the optimal use of your Echo Auto.

Important

Note that before every drive you will need to make sure that your car stereo is set to Bluetooth or auxiliary; and you'll need to adjust the volume on your phone and stereo.

Troubleshooting Echo Auto Setup

If Echo Auto doesn't connect right away here's what you can try...

- Unplug the power cable for about 45 second, then plug in again

- Echo Auto should automatically show the orange color going side to side on the LED bar (which signifies Setup mode); if not, then press the Action button for 8 seconds until you see iT

- Then go back into the Alexa App on your phone selecting **Devices > Add Device > Amazon Echo > Echo Auto** and following the prompts again.

Troubleshooting Echo Auto Bluetooth Connection

You might find, like me, that sometimes Echo Auto disconnects from Bluetooth for no apparent reason! This is super annoying, because there is no way of reconnecting without going manual – not something you can easily do when driving!

If this happens repeatedly, then I suggest connecting your Echo Auto to your car stereo via the auxiliary port instead. If it just happens intermittently, then here are some things to try (in no particular order):

- Force close the Alexa App, and then launch it again.

- If that doesn't work then unplug the micro-USB power cable from your Echo Auto; wait about 30 seconds, and then plug it back in.

- If you have an Android phone, try turning on Airplane mode on your phone. Wait 45 seconds, and then turn it off. If you have an iPhone then try turning off Bluetooth on your phone and then turn it on.

- Another option is to turn off and then restart your smartphone.

- Finally, you could try going into your Echo Auto settings in the Alexa App and forget the device. Then go to your phone's Bluetooth settings to check if your phone is connected to Echo Auto and then unpair that connection; then unplug the micro-USB power cable from your Echo Auto; wait 45 seconds, and then plug it back in; open the Alexa App and complete setup again.

If all else fails you can go into the Settings in the Alexa App and force a factory reset for the Echo Auto and then start again!

Add a Second Alexa-enabled device (optional)

If you have a passenger who also has the Alexa App on their phone, then you can add that person to your setup parameters. Once you have your Echo Auto successfully connected to your phone's App, press and hold the Action button for 8 seconds to activate pairing mode and then go through the setup in Devices again.

Access the Alexa App on your computer, and sign in (optional)

This used to be my preferred way to use the Alexa App, as I like the larger view. The App address for your computer is: alexa.amazon.com. However, in recent months, I have realized that the Alexa App is not identical on different platforms. That is to say the layout, interface and some of the features are different depending on whether you're looking at the App on a PC or on a mobile phone.

Throughout this book, if necessary I will point out differences in the interface, as there are times when setting features up on the Alexa App is easier to do manually on your PC, but I strongly recommend using your mobile phone as that is the most popular way of accessing the Alexa App and how you'll be using it when you're in your car.

Create your Voice Profile (optional)

You will of course know that Alexa can recognize any voice that speaks to her, but did you know that you are able to teach Alexa to recognize your particular voice and use that feature to link to these services for a personalized Alexa experience? Voice profiles can be set for up to 10 people on most Alexa-enabled devices. Once you have a Voice Profile you can enjoy these enhanced features:

- Flash Briefing, Alexa will give you news updates that are linked to your personal flash briefing choices.

- Prime Music Unlimited family plan users, say "Play music" and Alexa will play music tailored to your specific Music Unlimited profile.

- Voice Purchasing, when you have a Voice Profile saved then you don't need to give Alexa your voice purchasing code to proceed with a purchase.

- Calling & Messaging, when using this feature Alexa will automatically call or message people listed only on your personal contacts.

To create your **Voice Profile**, simply ask Alexa to "Learn my voice", and then follow the vocal prompts from Alexa. You will be asked to repeat 10 phrases like "Alexa, order pink pajamas" and "Amazon, feed the cat". And then, when she's done with setting up your profile, Alexa says, "Nice to meet you"!

To create a **Voice Profile** for a different person, not listed on your account at Set Up, tap on **Settings** and then scroll down to log out; then sign back in to your Alexa App account, where under your name you should see the option **I'm someone else**. Click or tap on this and follow the instructions again to create a different personal profile. Then you can ask Alexa to "learn my voice" again, using the new profile.

Note that if you've already created an Amazon Household (see below) then members of the Household can say "Switch accounts" and then ask Alexa to "Learn my voice".

To delete a Voice Profile, select **Settings > Accounts > Your Voice > Forget my voice** and confirm.

Create an Amazon Household (optional)

This is another setup feature you might want to wait till later to do, if at all.

If there are other Amazonians in your household — your literal or figurative "household" — you might want to share capabilities such as being able to listen to each other's music. You can explore the benefits and how-to's of Amazon Households in more detail by following the instructions manually below or going to www.amazon.com/myh/manage.

- On Amazon.com hover over ***Accounts & Lists*** near the top of the page

- Select "***Your Account***"

- In the "***Shopping programs and rentals***" box (bottom right), select ***Amazon Households*** to go to the ***Manage Your Household / Your Amazon Household Benefits page***

- Select "***Add an Adult***," and follow the instructions including providing their login information, so they will have to give it to you or be there with you to type it in

- And/or select "***Add a Child***," Create and Save their Profile, and follow the link to ***Manage Your Content and Devices*** to determine the content they can access

2: Meet the Alexa App

*For any voice command you read in this chapter be sure to use
your wake word ("Alexa", "Amazon", etc) first.*

Now that setup is complete, you'll get the most utility from the Echo Auto and complete tasks more quickly if you know your way around the Alexa App. We will refer to **Settings** several times here. They are a part of the App, but there's so much information to share about **Settings** that it has its <u>own chapter</u>. It's inevitable that some information will be covered in both places.

Amazon calls Alexa the "brain behind" its Echo devices. Alexa is cloud-based, making it possible for Alexa and the Echo devices to continually be improved and updated. If you're worried about security, consider that it's likely that many of your accounts are already somewhere in the cloud — banking, credit cards, medical in addition to other Amazon accounts such as Prime or Drive. The same level of security used with that information is used with Alexa.

The App and your Voice

Most of what you can do via the Alexa App can also be done with voice. If you're listening to an Amazon music station, for example, you can select the Pause button on the App or simply say, "pause." In the remainder of this guide, we will occasionally note things you have to do manually, such as setting up certain parameters for Smart Home devices. But for the most part, assume you can accomplish the task with your voice, and give it a try.

There is also interplay between the App screen on your phone and your voice requests. For example, when you're listening to media, information about what your listening to will display on the **Now Playing** page of the App, or when you add an item to your **Shopping List**, you can consult the list on the relevant App page too.

A Word about Help & Feedback

The **Help & Feedback** page, accessible within the Alexa App, is discussed in detail later, but it's worth knowing before we get started that this section contains a wealth of information about all the topics discussed throughout the rest of this book.

The Alexa App Homepage

The Alexa App looks different depending on what you're using to view it.

On the tablet and mobile phone version of the App; no matter what page you are on, there are four icons at the bottom of the page:

- **Home** icon to take you back to the **Homepage** which is a trapezoid shape with two lines under it, I think it's supposed to represent the Cards (more about those later)

- **Communications** icon (a little speech bubble) to take you to the relevant pages of the App for making calls and sending messages, dropping-in and announcements.

- **Play** icon – a circle with a triangle inside - which takes you to the Music & Books pages.

- **Devices** icon (a little house with two switches inside) which takes you to the landing page for all Alexa-enabled devices, including Echo devices and any other smart home devices that are integrated into your Alexa system (discussed further later on).

If you ever access the Alexa App on your PC or a Mac you'll see that things are a little simpler: you'll see a Menu of App pages on the left and the current page on the right.

But as you'll be in your car, using the Echo Auto, we're going to be using the App on your phone, so this is the interface that we'll be discussing for most of the rest of the book.

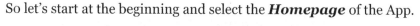

So let's start at the beginning and select the *Homepage* of the App.

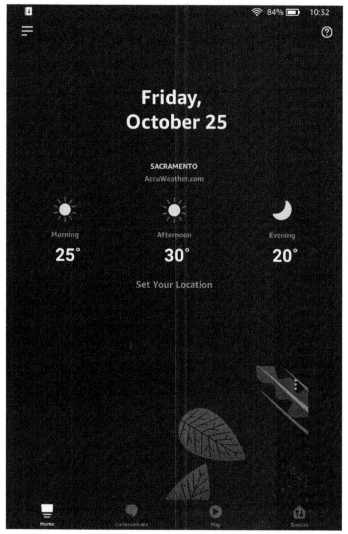

So, when you're on the *Homepage* on your mobile, what you'll see on your screen at the top are three horizontal bars on the left hand corner (when you tap on this you'll get a *Menu* of other options); a question mark icon that leads to the *Help & Feedback* section on the right hand corner; and a greeting (Good Morning, Good Afternoon etc...) in the middle and, if you enable a weather Skill, there will be your local weather report.

21

Below the greeting you'll be able to scroll upwards through a series of floating tabs that either take you to different pages of the App, offer information on new Skills or Things to Try, or – once you've started using Alexa – will show links to where you left off on you Audible book or the Music currently playing/ or last played.

These tabs act a bit like your activity history on the App. However, to get fuller details of your activity and to what Amazon call your "Cards" then go to **Menu > Activity**.

A Card is created with most verbal interactions with Alexa. The Card preserves the request and response from Alexa such as a music station or a forecast you requested, a Skill used or items you added to your shopping list.

Often these cards aren't of much interest, but as you'll discover later there are times when they are useful, like after you've asked for weather, movie or local business information. Some Cards offer options to help improve your Alexa experiences like **Search** options to find out more via Bing or Wikipedia, and to give **Voice Feedback** if Alexa didn't hear you correctly.

Finally, at the bottom of the **Homepage**, when media (songs, radio, podcasts, etc.) is loaded, a **Player** appears at the bottom of the Alexa App page and allows you to control that media manually. The **Player** appears at the bottom of the App regardless of what page you're on when viewing the App. It is discussed fully in the **Now Playing** section next.

3: The 'Now Playing' Page and Player

For any voice command you read in this chapter be sure to use your wake word ("Alexa", "Amazon", etc) first.

One of Alexa's most attractive features is its ability to play media from a wide range of sources.

I appreciate that you might not have anything to play yet and therefore much of this chapter might not make sense to you. If this is the case, feel free to skip ahead and return to this chapter when you are ready.

To access the **Now Playing** page on your mobile phone, when you have media playing tap on the **Player**, which loads on the bottom of whatever page you're viewing (the **Player** is always visible on every page of the mobile App when media plays, though it does sometimes take a little while to load).

The **Player** will then expand to show the full **Now Playing** page. This features an image of the media playing – for example an album cover image – plus an icon for the source such as iHeartRadio, Kindle audiobooks or a podcast on TuneIn to remind you where the media is coming from. And under those images, is the *media Player*.

To control the functions of the **Player** via Echo Auto, simply tell Alexa what you want to do, for example say, "pause," "resume," "play", "stop", "go back" or "go forward." And you can ask Alexa to change the volume with commands such as "volume seven" or "mute."

You can also manually tap or click any option on the Now Playing page. The Player always offers these control symbols:

- **Play/Pause, Go back, Go forward**
- **Volume bar:** Tap on the Loudspeaker icon to see the volume bar,

which you can set manually by swiping it left or right.

- **Progress bar:** This gives you the ability to change the place in the song or audiobook.

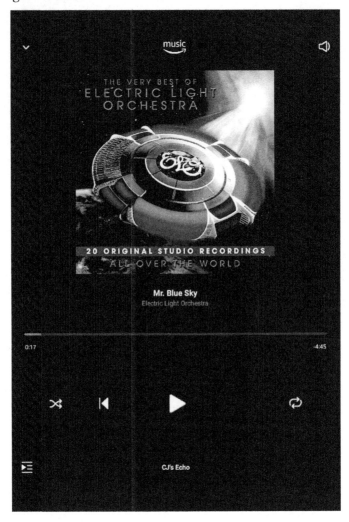

Depending on what type of media you are playing, additional options are shown on the player:

- **Shuffle:** Selecting the crossed arrows will cause the Queue to be played in random order.
- **Repeat:** Select the looping arrows to repeat the song or station when it is completed.

- **Forward/ Back 30 seconds:** This options displays for audio books, allowing you to flip forward or back a little if needed.

- **Playlist Queue/ Chapter:** Tapping on this square shaped icon that features a triangle and 4 lines will show you the list of chapters in your audiobook, or the play order of the playlist you're listening to. Play anything from Queue or History by tapping/clicking it. Your choice will then become the audio content that is Now Playing.

Note that if you want to see your media *History* on your mobile, then either select the Alexa App *Homepage* or the Play icon at the bottom of the page (the circle with a triangle inside) and the top of the page will show your most recently played media.

CJ's Tips: Note that if you are playing a station and then select another media, the station might be canceled. I learned this by pausing a station and asking for my news *Flash Briefing* (explained later but found in *Settings* if you want to explore it before we get to it).

The station did not resume, even at my request. Stations are not canceled if you ask for your weather forecast, something from Wikipedia or a simple question. The station volume is reduced while Alexa fulfills the request. I'm still learning which requests cancel stations and which don't. If a station gets canceled, and I want to continue listening, it's right there in *History* where I can pick up where I left off.

As mentioned above, if any of this is confusing right now then read on and return to this chapter once you have started playing some audio.

4: Songs by the Millions — Music

For any voice command you read in this chapter be sure to use your wake word ("Alexa", "Amazon", etc) first.

It's difficult to beat Alexa for ease and convenience for playing music from a diverse range of sources. But working out how to find and set up these different sources is not always that obvious!

Start by locating where all the music services are! On the Alexa App on your mobile phone, at the bottom you'll see a round icon with a triangle inside, the **Play** icon; tap on this to go to the **Music & Books** landing page.

On this page you will see any Amazon Music, Audible and Kindle ebooks that you already own and have recently played/ viewed. This area will be blank if you haven't used any of those media yet. For example, when I first downloaded the Alexa App, I already had some Kindle ebooks, so that's what I saw on the landing page; when I then set up an Audible and Amazon Prime Music account, I subsequently found my music and audio books listed here too.

Next, near the top of the **Music & Books** landing page you will see the word **Browse** – tap on this to see the different sources of Music that can be connected to your Alexa, such as Amazon My Music, Amazon Prime Music, Spotify, TuneIn and so on.

Finally, as you scroll down the page you will see a number of suggestions of things you might like to do, for example, "Link to your favorite streaming services", click on those suggestions to explore the option further.

So now let's look at the Music services you can connect to via Alexa in more detail:

My Music Library/ My Amazon Music

After selecting **Music & Books > Browse Music** you will see the label **My Amazon Music**. Tap on this to see **My Music Library**.

To be clear, this section of the Alexa App is where you access YOUR personal music collection of music from the Amazon music services that you've subscribed to; the next section, Amazon Prime Music, is where you can access ALL music available from Amazon.

The order seemed logically backwards to me when **My Music Library** was sparse, but now that I have a large Library of music, it makes sense. I access what I already have more often than I want to browse what else is available.

As mentioned above, your account's My Music Library will be populated with music that has been:

- Purchased from Amazon.

- Selected in the form of a Playlist from Amazon Prime and Amazon Music Unlimited subscriptions.

CJ's Tips: By the way the Amazon Music app (https://amzn.to/2ElWBci) for your desktop computer is Amazon's equivalent of the iTunes app. Once you have it installed you can play all the music in your Amazon Music account on your PC or Mac just like you probably do on iTunes already.

So, now let's explore the *My Music Library* further.

Firstly, right under the words My Music Library, you may be asked to select the device you want to play music on (only relevant if you have more than one Alexa-enabled device.)

You may also have the option to select the music Library you want to access. If you have set up an Amazon Household, you can access Libraries of household members too. An Amazon Household can include up to two adults, though each must have an Amazon account, and up to four children. Creating and managing an Amazon Household is done through your Amazon account. Here again are brief instructions and options for Amazon Households:

1. Hover over Accounts & Lists near the top of the page on Amazon.com

2. Select Your Account.

3. In the Shopping programs and rentals box, select Amazon Households to go to the Manage Your Household / Your Amazon Household Benefits page.

4. Select Add an Adult, and follow the instructions including providing their login information, so they will have to give it to you or be there with you to type it in.

5. And/or select Add a Child, Create and Save their Profile, and follow

the link to Manage Your Content and Devices to determine the content they can access.

Here is a direct link: www.amazon.com/myh/manage

Search Your Amazon Music Library

When you're in your car, using your Echo Auto, you're going to only be using your voice to ask Alexa for the songs of the playlist you want to play. But below I'll outline how to search your Music Library manually in case your passenger wants to search for songs (or for when you're not driving).

CJ Tips: In my experience, it helps to be as specific as possible when asking for music, such as, "Play Bruce Springsteen Born to Run from My Music Library," or "Play Bruce Springsteen Born to Run from Amazon Prime Music." Once you have a few different music services set up it helps Alexa if you let her know exactly which service you want the music to come from. I will talk about setting Default Music Services later to make this process even easier.

Search manually: Use the search box to find songs or albums more quickly in your Library. As you type the search word, a list of results will begin to populate and gradually narrow the more of the term you complete.

The next row is a menu of tabs: *Playlists/ Artists/ Albums/ Songs/ Genres*. Using them is a very straightforward process, so just a few comments will suffice for each.

Playlists: There are three sections here:

- **Auto Playlists:** Purchased — a list of all the songs you've purchased from Amazon, which in time might become a very long and eclectic list; and Recently Added — which includes recently imported playlists and a list of songs purchased in the last month or so.

- **Your Playlists:** These are playlists that you can create within the Amazon Prime Music service.

- **Prime Playlists:** These are preselected playlists that are available on Amazon Prime Music. If you don't have an Amazon Prime membership, then you won't see anything here. If you do, then it's time to add some of these Prime Playlists to your Music Library (see instructions below)!

- **Artists/ Albums/ Songs/ Genres:** These tabs all function the same, and you can find the music you want in two ways: scroll down through the alphabetical list at the left or jump down to its location using the #ABCDEFG, etc., list. Of course, you can also just ask Alexa to play the music you want.

Now let's look at all the streaming services you can connect to from the Alexa App.

Amazon Prime Music

After selecting **Music & Books > Browse Music** you will see the icon for Prime Music, which is the word music in lower case with the Amazon swoosh arrow underneath.

For this section to be relevant, you'll need a subscription to Amazon Prime and/or Amazon Music Unlimited.

Prime Music: This option is available as part of Amazon's standard monthly Prime membership deal, to be clear, you need to have the Prime membership deal to benefit.

- **Benefits:** stream 2 million songs in Prime Music and a long list of shipping, shopping and media benefits that can be viewed on Amazon.

- **Standard annual:** $119/year, after 30-day free trial.

- **Standard monthly:** $12.99/month, after a 30-day free trial.

There is also a student plan for $6.49/month or $59/year; and a plan for those who qualify for an EBT or Medicaid card, $5.99/ month.

Amazon Music Unlimited: If you do not wish to have a full Prime membership, then you can still access Amazon Music with this offer.

- "Unlimited access to tens of millions of songs" according to Amazon.

- New members get the first month free and then switch to a paid-for plan; Individual plans are currently $7.99/ month, whilst a family plan is $14.99/month which can be used by up to 6 members. Annual memberships both for individuals and families are also available.

- There is also a specific single device plan for use with an Amazon Echo or a Fire TV device for $3.99/ month. And a student plan for just $4.99/ month.

CJ's Tips: For what it's worth, my recommendation is getting a Prime membership since it offers so many other benefits, and if you then don't find enough of the kind of music you enjoy, consider adding a Music Unlimited subscription. Again, you can manage all music subscriptions from this here: www.amazon.com/music/settings

Amazon Music Unlimited HD: Launched in September 2019 to coincide with the launch of the new high-fidelity smart speaker, Echo Studio. This is a further tier of music provision from Amazon with over 50 million songs available in High Definition (HD) or Ultra High Definition (ultra HD). If you are a serious music buff, this is an option with considering. New users get 90 days free and then switch to a paid-for plan. At the time of writing the payment options available were:

- Amazon Music Unlimited subscribers: an additional $5 per month (Individual or Family plans only)

- Prime members: an additional $12.99 per month

- General Amazon customer (neither Prime members nor Amazon Music Unlimited subscriber): $14.99 per month

Search your Amazon Prime Music

Once you have your Prime music subscription you can return to the Alexa App (***Music & Books > Browse > Amazon Prime Music***) and explore. The options are labeled in two categories, ***Stations*** and ***Playlists***.

Stations: Amazon's Stations are music streams based on either a particular artist, era of music, or genre of music. Theoretically, if you choose a Station – just like the radio in the olden days – you will get that type of music on an endless stream. This is a good way to search for music in line with your preferences.

- **All Stations:** This section has two categories to browse, and when you make a selection, the Station begins to play. Popular Genres & Artists stations include Classical Focus, Top Pop, Smooth Jazz, Lullabies and other broad categories. Each of the All Artists (A-Z) stations brings together the very best music from across the band or artist's career. Try this feature for yourself, of course, but I rarely use it. There is no search function, and scrolling down thousands of artists is impractical.

- **Genres:** This is a more reasonable way to locate music you like, but you must go two levels deep to choose stations. Search categories including Featured, Pop, Country, Classic Rock, Christian, Alternative, Reggae, Clean, World, R&B, Classical and many more – even Christmas! Choose a genre and, you are given the list of subgenre "stations". For example, choosing the Classical genre gives you the choice of dozens of stations like Baroque, Classical Piano, Classical Piano, etc., and popular artists like Yo-Yo Ma, the Emerson String Quartet and Hilary Hahn.

Playlists: Amazon's Playlists are curated "albums" of music that have been put together by Amazon's team. Like the stations they are categorized according to genre or music era or artist, but in this case there will be a finite selection of tracks – for example 50 Great Feel-Good Classics. More than 1,700 Amazon Music Playlists have been curated, and the number is growing, so give yourself a day off to have a good look around!

You can simply click on a Station or a Playlist shown on the Alexa App pages to have Alexa play it; or when you know the title of the Playlist, you can just ask Alexa, for example: "Play 90s Dance Anthems".

However, to avoid too much searching around, you might prefer to add

Add Prime Playlists to My Music Library

There are two ways to add Prime Playlists:

Manually via Amazon.com:

- Go to your ***Amazon Prime Music online*** (music.amazon.com)

- Browse ***Playlists*** by clicking on the link at the top of the left hand side menu and continue finessing your options until you find the Playlist that interests you.

- Hover or tap a ***Playlist*** to see your options:

- Select the ***+ sign*** to add the entire list to your ***My Music Library*** "sight unseen," or later the X sign to remove it.

- Choose the ***Play*** icon to listen to the list, or later, the ***Pause*** icon to pause it; and then add it if you like it as above.

- **Select the three dots to:**

  - **Share the list:** Copy the link, copy the page code to embed elsewhere,

  - **email the link or share** it on Facebook or Twitter.

  - **Open the Playlist** to view how long it is, number of songs in the list, who curated the list and what its reviews are. There, you can also just choose individual songs form the list to add to your Music Library.

By Voice via the Alexa App:

- First go into the Alexa App to ***Music & Books > Amazon Prime Music > Playlists*** and find a Playlist you want to add.

- Click/tap the playlist to start it playing.

- Once it's playing you can open up the Now Playing page by tapping on the Player at the bottom of the page, and then you can click the Queue/Chapter icon (a square icon with a triangle and four lines) to see all the tracks in that Playlist.

- If you like what you see, then ask "Alexa, add this playlist to my library" and Alexa will do just that!

Once you've added Prime Playlists to your Music Library, when you next go into the Alexa App you'll see the Prime Playlists listed in the My Music Library pages.

CJ's Tips: Every track you hear on a Prime Playlist or Station comes from an album that is also available for you to listen to free as a Prime member. However, adding an album to your Music Library may require a little bit of detective work.

Here's an example... you hear the song "Don't" by Ed Sheeran on a Prime Playlist and decide you would like to listen to the whole album that the song comes from.

- First go online to Amazon Prime Music by going to music.amazon. com in the browser of your desktop computer.

- Second search "Don't Ed Sheeran" in the search box at the top of the page and hit enter.

- Third, your results will be shown so scroll down to Prime Songs and when you see the song "Don't, Ed Sheeran" click the three vertical dots to the right of the track. A pop up window will appear giving you further options and one of those options should be *View Album.*

- Fourth, go ahead and click *View Album* and you will be shown the entire album that the track is from plus the option to + *Add to My Music*, and clicking that will add the album (in this example the album is called "X (Wembley Edition)") to your music library.

Now you're all set and can just ask "Alexa, play the album X from my Music Library".

Spotify

With 232 million users and 108 million subscribers, www.spotify.com

is one of the largest music streaming platforms. While Spotify has a free subscription, a premium account is required for use with Alexa. That's Spotify's choice. The current cost of a premium account is $9.99/ month for those who have not tried Premium before. Besides using their service with Alexa, benefits include the ability to download music to your devices to listen offline, skip songs you don't like as often as you want, play any song and listen without ads.

To create an account, choose an email address to link to, a password, user name and payment method, which can be a credit card or PayPal. If you choose PayPal, Spotify will connect to PayPal, and you might have to sign in. Once on PayPal, you will select which payment associated with your account you want to use.

Linking Spotify to Alexa: Once you have a premium account, select *Spotify* from the *Music & Books > Browse Music* tab, and choose: *Link your account > Authorize the Account* (If asked)

A new window will open where you will have to authorize the connection of Alexa to your Spotify account. Once you do that, return to the Alexa App where you will be asked whether you want to make Spotify your default music service. If you want to change that later, it can be done at *Settings > Music & Media > Choose default music services.* There, you can select a Default music library and a Default station service.

If you want to unlink your Spotify account, select *Settings > Music & Media > Spotify* and *Unlink Account from Alexa*. On that page, you can also go to Spotify to Manage Spotify Settings such as upgrade to a Premium for Family account, view and edit your profile or see when the next Renew date is.

Using Spotify on Echo Auto: If you've made Spotify your Default music service, you can use your voice or the Spotify app to play music from the service. For voice, simply request music from your favorite artist, and Alexa will play it. If it's not the Default service, you'll have to say, "Play Selena Gomez on Spotify," for example. As usual, the Player will appear on the *Now Playing* page and at the bottom of any other page you're viewing. Then you can control Player functions using your voice – say, "Play", "Skip", "Shuffle" or manually when appropriate.

Pandora

Pandora is often referred to as an online radio pioneer, having been launched at the dawn of Internet radio streaming services back in 2000. Currently Pandora is only available in the USA. But it's popularity is as good as ever, with over 160 million users, and over 30 million tracks available, it's safe to say that Pandora will be here for a while longer.

One of the benefits of Pandora, for our purposes, is that you can use Alexa with a free Pandora account, which I do. If you already have an account, you can skip to Linking Alexa to Pandora below.

There are currently three membership levels, see www.pandora.com:

- **Pandora Free:** Free; Ad-supported radio; Personalized stations.

- **Pandora Plus:** $4.99/month; 30-day free trial; Ad-free Personalized stations; Better audio; Offline radio.

- **Pandora Premium:** $9.99/month; 60-day free trial; Ad-free; Create new stations and playlists rather than personalizing existing stations; Better audio; No limit on skips and replays; Download music to other devices.

Select the level you prefer, and you'll be taken to an account signup page. Even if you select a free trial for a paid subscription, providing an email address and password on the first page will immediately begin a free account.

Linking Pandora to Alexa: Back on the Alexa App, select *Pandora from Music & Books > Browse Music*. Then, choose: *Link your account > Authorize the link*

Using Pandora on Echo Auto: If you haven't used Pandora before, it's worth exploring and setting things up manually first; then you can use voice control with your Echo Auto to ask Alexa to play music from Pandora.

So, manually, once Alexa and Pandora are linked, you'll have two options on the Pandora page on the Alexa App.

- Choose + **Create Station**, and enter an artist, genre or track to search or scroll through the **Browse Genre** section to view more than 60 genres from standards like Rock, Alternative, Classical, Hip Hop/Rap, Instrumental, Comedy and Decades to niche categories like GameDay, Mexico, Rainy Day, Pandora Local and Driving.

- Browse and choose one of the stations listed below **My Stations**, a list that will populate once you start adding stations or will be displayed immediately if you link to an existing account. Toggle Sort by date (date added) and Sort by A-Z to view the My Stations list. The first entry will always be Shuffle to mix the list randomly. There is a scroll bar on the side of the list of My Stations, but as I've said, it is difficult to see, being black on dark gray.

Now that you have some stations in your Pandora My Stations section, you can use Alexa voice controls to have them play via your Echo Auto. As always, the Player will appear at the bottom of the Alexa App page on your phone, or you can tap to get to get to the **Now Playing** page if you want to control the music manually.

CJ's Tips: I like Pandora, they have some great stations and I have no problem asking Alexa for a station based around an artist like, "Alexa, play Adele on Pandora," but things get more problematic when I ask for a themed playlist like "Alexa, play Laid Back Brunch on Pandora." There were many stations like this that got no response from Alexa even when I set Pandora as my default station service.

If you encounter this problem, then the solution unfortunately is to revert to manual! You need to go back to **Music & Books > Browse Music > Pandora > Browse Genre** on the Alexa App and start a playlist playing. It will immediately be added as one of your stations and will appear under My Stations. Now try again to ask for it with your voice and you should have no problem. Not an ideal solution for when you're driving!

iHeartRadio

This radio network and Internet radio platform offers an immense amount of content including music and podcasts provided by 800 iHeartRadio partner stations in the US, more than 1,000 artist stations and a range of other media.

There are three membership levels:

- **iHeartRadio:** No cost, but you're limited to choosing a local radio station or curated stations built around well-known artists but including similar artists.

- **iHeartRadio Plus:** $4.99/month through Alexa; Play any song on demand; Unlimited skips; Save songs to create a single playlist; Replay songs from live radio and custom stations.

- **iHeartRadio All Access:** $9.99 through Alexa; Everything offered in Plus; Unlimited access to millions of songs; Listen offline on iOS and Android versions, but not yet on Alexa; Create as many playlists as you like.

I tried All Access but settled on the free iHeartRadio account simply because I've got so many other music choices that I don't need a paid service. If you start out with a free account, select the ***Upgrade Now*** tab on iHeartRadio at any time to try one of the paid plans.

Linking iHeartRadio to Alexa: Select ***iHeartRadio*** from the ***Music & Books*** > ***Browse Music*** page and then ***Link Your Account.*** Authorize the link to an existing account or create a free or upgraded account with personal and payment information.

Using iHeartRadio on Echo Auto: You can use voice control to ask Alexa to find music for you via iHeartRadio. Again, you need to be very exact when asking Alexa for something from iHeartRadio, especially when asking for a radio station. I find saying "Alexa, play 102.7 KIIS-FM Los Angeles" is a bit of a mouthful and can be hard to remember precisely.

CJ's Tips: I prefer to save my iHeartRadio stations as favorites manually (see below) and then I find that Alexa is much more likely to understand what I am requesting.

Explore iHeartRadio manually: In the Alexa App go to *Music & Books > Browse Music > iHeartRadio*. The homepage has a search box where you can type in keywords including an artist's name, genre or city, for example. Searches return results related to your keyword, and they're divided into four categories:

- **Stations** — Artist Stations are titled after well-known artists to give you an idea of the flavor of the music, but each station includes songs from a range of artists. I'm currently listening to the station called Adele. The song Queue includes Rihanna, Ed Sheeran, Lorde, Ellie Goulding, OneRepublic and others in addition to Adele.

- **Songs** — Singles by title or group name related to the keyword.

- **Artists** — Bands, solo acts, choirs, etc. with names related to the keyword.

- **Talk Shows** — Shows and podcasts with names related to the keyword.

When you find station or shows that you like you can choose them as favorites. This is crucial for easy use of iHeartRadio via Echo Auto!

Your second option to locate music is the Browse section with three categories to look through:

- **Live Radio:** 800+ radio stations from around the country.

- **Shows:** These are mostly podcasts and the 20+ categories include Business & Finance, Comedy, Crime, Entertainment, Politics, Spirituality and Sports. Categories contain a dozen to more than 100 show options.

- **Favorites:** As mentioned above, you have the option to select any station or show as a favorite, and it will be saved here for easy locating later, though it might not show up immediately.

Manually select any Station and it will begin to play. Once playing, the content can be controlled on the **Player** or the ***Now Playing page*** or with your voice.

TuneIn

TuneIn is one of the oldest streaming services, founded in 2002. Today, its specialties are Music, News, Sports and Talk, and TuneIn carries local, national and international content. Free and Premium accounts are available:

- **TuneIn Radio:** Free; Ad-supported. Stream 100,000 radio stations covering the range of styles.

- **TuneIn Premium:** $9.99/month; Ad-free. Stream 100,000 radio stations, 600 ad-free music stations, audio books and podcasts; Listen to live coverage of sports events including play-by-play of every NFL, MLB, NBA, and NHL game and more.

- **TuneIn Live on Alexa:** This is a specific deal that was launched in March 2018 for customers who either have an Alexa-enabled device or an Amazon Prime membership. It is effectively an add-on to the Free TuneIn offer, and allows you to access the live coverage of sports events including play-by-play of every NFL, MLB, NBA, and NHL game and more. The price is currently $2.99/ month ($3.99/ per month for non-prime members that have an Alexa-enabled device). Note that this offer is mainly aimed at owners of Amazon's Echo products, and is not currently fully integrated with some third-party Alexa-enabled devices such as the Sonos One smart speaker.

Linking TuneIn to Alexa: On the ***Music & Books*** > ***Browse Music*** page, select ***TuneIn*** > ***Link your account*** > ***Authorize the link***. You can create an account there by providing the standard information, choosing the membership level you prefer and providing payment information if you choose Premium.

Using TuneIn on Echo Auto: We found using TuneIn with Alexa a little hit-and-miss. Even if you know what you want, Alexa might have difficulty with your request if you use voice. For example, I said, "Play ESPN Outside the Lines," a popular show. Alexa replied, "Do you want me to add an outside station to your TuneIn account?" No, but thanks for asking. The request, "Outside the Lines, ESPN" had Alexa take me to a random ESPN station!

This again demonstrates that the more content available through Alexa, the more specific you'll need to be if using voice, and your request still might not produce the desired results. The best bet is when you're not driving, to go into the TuneIn pages via Alexa App manually, locate a station, show or podcast that you want to return to, and "Favorite" it immediately.

Explore TuneIn manually: The TuneIn homepage is set up much like the iHeartRadio page with a search box and more specific means of searching.

- Using the **Search Box** returns uncategorized results, unless you type in the exact name of the show or station you want, and that's a disadvantage compared with iHeartRadio. You're given a very long list of results to scroll through, and so I rarely use the function. Obviously, the more specific your search can be, the better results you'll get. You might have to try several searches using differing words or groups of words to find what you're looking for.

- The **Browse** function is more successful, and here TuneIn has the edge on iHeartRadio. Select from:

  — Favorites, which is empty at first but will be populated as you "Favorite" content you like.

  — Local Radio based on where you've given as your location at **Settings > Device Location > Edit.**

  — Trending list of stations and shows currently popular.

  — Music that is divided into 40+ subcategories for decade and musical genre.

  — Talk with 30+ genre subcategories.

  — Sports with 20+ subcategories including popular US, European and world sports, fantasy football and podcasts.

— News with a short list of trending shows from popular sources such as NPR, CNN and BBC, and two expandable subcategories: More Shows and Recent Episodes.

— By Location allows you to find news from continents and regions around the globe.

— By Language, with more than 90 languages offered.

— Podcasts broken into Music, Sports and Talk categories with a range of subcategories in each.

Once you choose a **Category** > **Subcategory** from **Search** or **Browse** results, a list of shows will be displayed for you to select from. Using the Alexa App for this purpose, rather than voice, is the best method.

SiriusXM

SiriusXM started by offering satellite radio services and has expanded into online radio where it's a good fit for Alexa. There are 70+ music channels, 20+ talk and entertainment channels, 10+ sports channels, 15+ news and issues channels, traffic and weather, Latin, Comedy and more.

Alexa's relationship with SiriusXM is different than it is with iHeartRadio, TuneIn, Spotify and Pandora. SiriusXM is an Alexa Skill, so the platform isn't supported to the same extent as the other services. We'll cover Alexa Skills in detail in a later chapter. It being a Skill might be why the Alexa & SiriusXM connection is more problematic. I suggest you read the information on the SiriusXM page on the Alexa App for an overview and for ratings from users.

The service currently has 3/5 Stars or 60% favorable after about 1,000 ratings. Problems include connecting with and accessing SiriusXM, Alexa not recognizing login information or saying it is wrong, and linking to SiriusXM causing user's Echo devices to stop working entirely. The last issue is especially concerning, though I haven't experienced it. My experience has been that Customer Service at Sirius isn't up to speed about linking Amazon Alexa with SiriusXM at this writing.

Here's something else that might deter you from opening a new SiriusXM account, and it is due to it being a Skill rather than a fully supported service: you can't search or browse SiriusXM from the Alexa App. Using voice is the only current option. You must know the name of what you want to hear or use trial and error to find what you want. I said, "Play football on SiriusXM." The first response was, "What do you want to hear?" When I asked again, the reply was, "I couldn't find a station called 'football' on SiriusXM."

Linking SiriusXM to Alexa: If you want to proceed and have a SiriusXM account:

- Scroll to *SiriusXM* on the *Music & Books > Browse Music* page.

- Select *Enable* and follow the prompts. If you do not have an account and still think it's worth checking out after the caveats given, sign up for an All Access trial or paid account at www.siriusxm.com/amazonalexa

- Sirius will send you a confirmation email.

- Select the link included to set up your password for your SiriusXM account and return to login to begin.

- Then, come back to the Alexa App to select Enable and make the connection.

CJ's Tips: If you are exploring the Alexa App via your computer, make sure popups are enabled in your browser or system settings. You might have to restart your computer after enabling popups to apply the change. The SiriusXM Skill can also be Enabled on Amazon's site here: https://amzn.to/2ONRuFO

Deezer

Deezer is one of the new kids on the block in the US market, but has been around for quite a while in Europe having been created in 2006 in Paris. A cross between Spotify and TuneIn, Deezer is an internet-based music streaming service. The service currently boasts of having 53 million licensed titles in its library, with more than 30,000 stations 14 million active users per month and 6 million paying subscribers as of April 3, 2018.

To use Deezer with Alexa, you will need a Deezer Premium + account which costs $9.99 / month. Then, similar to SiriusXM, the Deezer service on Alexa is provided via the Deezer Skill. So once you have registered your Deezer Premium + account on the Deezer website, you can then access the Alexa app and activate the Deezer skill (as you would for other Skills). When you do this, you will be prompted to link Alexa to your Deezer Premium account.

At the time of writing, the Deezer skill did not have many positive reviews, and an overall rating of 2.5/5 stars. In my opinion, there are still a number of bugs that need to be ironed out before the Deezer skill on Alexa is a viable contender.

Other Music/ Radio Skills

It is worth noting that there are many other radio stations that are offering specific Skills on the Alexa App allowing you to connect directly to their online stream, from national sports coverage on CBS Sports to local radio stations such as Radio Milwaukee. If you have a favorite radio station it might be worth checking if it has an Alexa skill so you can enable it and enjoy via voice control. Go to **Skills > Search all skills** on the Alexa App to explore the possibilities.

Setting Default Music Service

I've mentioned Default Music Services a couple of times now so let's discuss them more fully. To find this option go to **Menu > Settings > Music** and then scroll down to Account settings and select ***Default services***

You'll then see your current options (they may change) include setting a default music library and a default station service.

Once a default has been chosen Alexa will always search that service first when you make a request like "Alexa, play Avril Lavigne". Choose your preferred library and station service based on which sources you use the most, and remember that if you want music from a different source you will have to state that resource in your request, for example, "Alexa, play Avril Lavigne from iHeartRadio".

One quirk to watch out for, I have Amazon Prime Music set as my default library and station service, but if I want to hear something from My Music Library I still have to specify it in my request and be really specific if I want a particular album.

Example I asked Alexa "Play Earth, Wind & Fire" and, instead of tracks by the band Earth, Wind & Fire, Alexa started playing a track called "Earth, Wind and Fire" by Miguel from Prime Music. I tried again "Alexa, play Earth, Wind & Fire from My Music Library" and things got better as Alexa played a range of the band's tracks from across My Music Library, but I specifically wanted to hear the Greatest Hits album so I had to try once more, "Alexa, play Earth, Wind & Fire Greatest Hits" before I got exactly what I wanted.

I just relay this fascinating anecdote to demonstrate that setting a default music service is still no substitute for getting into the habit of being as specific as possible with all your requests!

CJ's Tips: Remember, once some music is playing via your Echo Auto you can control it with your voice with some pretty obvious commands like "What's this song", "Pause", "Turn down the volume", "Resume", "Next song", "Repeat this song" etc.

But did you know you could be a bit more adventurous than that? Try asking, "Play road trip music" or "Play music I can dance to" and see what Alexa comes up with!

5: Tell Me a Story — Books

For any voice command you read in this chapter be sure to use your wake word ("Alexa", "Amazon", etc) first.

I must admit that I was not really that keen on the idea audiobooks (though I do love reading), but actually trying out the option on my Echo at home whilst relaxing one evening has been something of a revelation, and one that I am now enjoying in my car too! Here's how you too can listen to a vast library of written material using your Echo Auto:

Audible

Audible is an Amazon company, and its offerings have been significantly expanded in the last few years from just audiobooks to podcasts and original content that sounds more like a radio drama than a book because it is written for voice and read by a cast. For example, the X-Files: Cold Cases audiobook is four hours of material adapted from the series and read by David Duchovny, Gillian Anderson and other original and new actors. Audible books are read in the original reader's voice, not Alexa's.

Currently, Audible boasts over 425,000 titles in their English language catalogue ranging across a wide selection of genres, so there is plenty to choose from!

At the time of writing, the standard gold monthly Audible plan includes:

- 30-day Free Audible trial with two Audible Originals and one free audiobook to keep (Audible Originals are exclusive titles that produced in the Audible studios).

- $14.95/month after, with the option to cancel at any time.

- 3 books per month – one standard audiobook and two Audible

Originals - and all books chosen during your subscription are yours to keep forever even if you cancel.

- 30% discount off additional audiobooks.

- If you don't like a book, you have an exchange period for trading it for another.

- Free Audible app that allows you to listen on all your devices.

- Whispersync syncing that keeps your place in an audiobook even when you switch devices.

Get Started with Audible: Here's how to get started with your Audible account

- Sign up for a free trial at www.audible.com

- Sign into your Amazon account.

- Choose *Existing Payment Method* (which will be indicated with its last 4 digits) or choose *Add New Payment Method* and complete its details

- Select *Start Your Membership*

- Select your free book.

- Cancel within 30 days to avoid being charged, if desired.

Connecting Audible to Alexa: Once your Audible account is established, it's time to integrate Alexa with Audible:

- In the Alexa App select the Play icon to get to *Music & Books*. The audio book will simply show up in the Audible section on this page, ready to be played.

Listen to Audible on Echo Auto: Here's how to enjoy your Audible audiobooks on your Echo Auto:

- Simply use your voice to ask for the book title, or say, "Read my Audible book," and Alexa will ask which book, or you can request it by title.

- For books in progress, say, "Resume my Audible book".

- Use voice for controls like pause, go forward, go back, go to chapter 7, read louder and similar requests.

- You can also say things like, "Stop reading in 15 minutes" and "Set a 15-minute sleep timer" to have Alexa end reading when you want.

- Note that the audiobook will also appear on your phone on the Alexa App Player and you can then use manual controls as well, when appropriate.

Kindle Books

Amazon's Kindle has been an innovative eBook reader since its introduction. Now you can listen to Kindle books with Alexa — no Kindle needed. However, you should note that Kindle books are read in Alexa's voice.

You can purchase Kindle books individually or choose a Kindle Unlimited. Here's what's currently offered:

- 30-day free Kindle Unlimited trial.

- Kindle Unlimited is $9.99/month and includes unlimited reading of 1 million book titles (new and recent books are not included) and magazines; note that not all of these million books are available to be listened to as audiobooks!

- Kindle books can also be borrowed, lent and rented. To find out more about these features visit https://amzn.to/2ytsbid

- With an Amazon Prime membership, you can select one Kindle First early release book and borrow one additional book free each month.

Getting Started with Kindle Books: Here's how to create a Kindle account

- If you love audiobooks, consider a Kindle Unlimited 30-day trial, and the books can also be read on a Kindle reader or Kindle for PC.

- To start a free trial, sign into your Amazon account from the Kindle Unlimited page (amzn.to/2Of9o6h)

- Choose Existing *Payment Method* (which will be indicated with its last 4 digits) or choose **Add New Payment Method** and complete its details, then select **Start Your Membership**.

- Cancel within 30 days to avoid being charged, if desired.

- If you don't want Kindle Unlimited, purchase, barrow, rent or select free Kindle books.

- If you already have a Kindle account, the books Alexa can read will show up in the Kindle section of the Alexa App.

Connecting Kindle Books to Alexa: Once you have some Kindle Books that Alexa can read in your Kindle account here's how to integrate Alexa with Kindle:

- In the Alexa App select the **Play** icon to get to **Music & Books**. Your book will simply show up in the Kindle Books section of on this page, ready to be played.

Listening to Kindle Books on Echo Auto: Here's how to enjoy your Kindle audiobooks on your Echo Auto:

Simply use your voice to ask for the book title, or say, "Read my Kindle book," and Alexa will ask which book, or you can request it by title.

For books in progress, say, "Resume my Kindle book".

Use voice for controls like pause, go forward, go back, go to chapter 7, read louder and similar requests.

You can also say things like, "Stop reading in 15 minutes" and "Set a 15-minute sleep timer" to have Alexa end reading when you want.

Note that the Kindle book will also appear on your phone on the Alexa App Player and you can then use manual controls as well, when appropriate.

Now that we've gone through all your audio entertainment options you might want to return to Chapter 3 about the **Now Playing** page to familiarize yourself with what that page of the Alexa App offers.

6: Write it Down & Get it Done — Lists

For any voice command you read in this chapter be sure to use your wake word ("Alexa", "Amazon", etc) first.

Alexa offers convenience you'll enjoy when making a Shopping List or To-do List. Both functions are explained in detail below. First note that manually on the Alexa App, you can tap on the Lists tab from the App Menu and you will see three options, at the top the words Create Lists (more about that later) and then Shopping and To-Do.

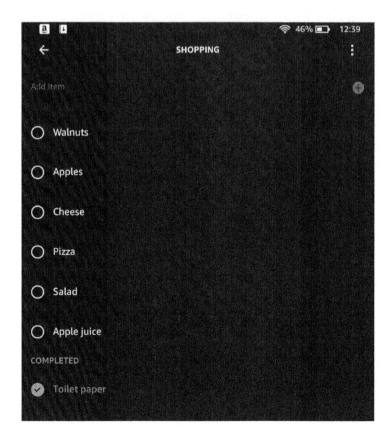

Shopping Lists

Creating and managing a shopping list to take with you on your mobile App is pretty convenient, and you might find the process fun too, as I do. Here are your options:

Create your Shopping List – Voice: For just one item say, "Add walnuts to the shopping list" regardless of the page showing on the Alexa App. Currently, Alexa seems only able to deal with adding one item at a time, so if you have more than one item for your list, then this series of commands works best: first say, "Add items to my shopping list" and Alexa will say "OK, what shall I add?", say, "Walnuts" (without the Wake Word), then Alexa will say, "I've added walnuts to your shopping list, anything else?", say the next item and the back and forth dialogue will continue until, when Alexa next says "...anything else?", you say "No".

Create your Shopping List – Manually: Select *Shopping List* from the Lists page, type things you want to buy into the *Add Item* + box at the top of the page, and select the + *sign* or tap *enter*.

Manage your Shopping List – Voice: Say "What's on my shopping list," and Alexa will read the list out to you, with the most recent item at the top. Then say, "Remove brown rice from my shopping list" or "Remove item number 7 from my shopping list" to take it off the list. Saying "Check off" instead of "Remove" works too. When you next check your list on the App, the removed items will be checked off and in the completed section of the list. Note that you will need to access the list manually via your PC or tablet etc., to actually fully delete the item from the list.

Manage your Shopping List – Manually: Swipe right to check off an item. It will then move automatically to the completed section of the list. Once in the completed section of the list you can then *swipe left* to either *Delete* the item off the list or *Restore* the item to the active shopping list. You can also just swipe left straight away to *Delete* or to search for the item on Amazon.

Hear your Shopping List: I say, "Shopping list" to hear it because efficiency appeals to me. If you're more conversational, say "What's on my shopping list," or anything similar. The Alexa voice recognition technology has its voice-recognition "ears" open for "shopping list" almost regardless of what else you say. Try it!

View your Shopping List Active and Completed on the App: When you check off an item it instantly appears underneath the "active" list under a heading title Completed; as mentioned before you can then swipe left to either delete or restore the item to your list.

To-do Lists

There are just a few differences when creating and managing this list compared to the Shopping List.

Create your To-do List – Voice: Simply say, "Add call doctor to the to-do list" regardless of the page showing on the Alexa App. Alternatively, say "Add item to my to-do list" and Alexa will say "OK, what can I add for you?" or something similar, then say "Call doctor" (without the Wake Word), and Alexa will confirm that she's done it. Currently, Alexa seems only able to deal with adding one item at a time to the To-do list; and unlike the Shopping List, there is no way of creating a dialogue series for adding more items to the list.

Create your To-do List – Manually: Select To-do from the Lists page, and type tasks into the Add Item + box at the top of the page

Manage your To-do List – Voice: Say "Remove repair the faucet from my to-do list" or "Remove item number 5 from my to-do list." Saying, "Check off" instead of "Remove" works too.

Manage your To-do List – Manually: Check off a completed task by selecting the box to its left, and a ✔ will appear in the box, the item will be ~~crossed out~~, and the ***Delete*** option will appear on the right. Click or tap the ***Delete*** option at right if you want to remove it from the list, or leave it there as a reminder it is complete

Hear your To-do List: Unfortunately, saying, "To-do list" won't deliver a reading of the list. Instead, Alexa will ask, "What can I add to your To-do list," or similar. You will have to say, "Read my," "Tell me my," or "What is on my" To-do list.

View your To-do List Active and Completed Tasks on the App:
This works the same as for the Shopping Lists described above.

Create Your Own List

A recent update to the Alexa App now allows you to create your very own list! You can create a list by voice or manually. By voice, just say "create a list" and then follow Alexa's prompts as she asks you what to call the list (example, "Birthday Party") and then what to put on the list... the list you create will work exactly the same way as the To-do list. I found it to be a handy option for making a guest list for my kid's birthday party.

Manually, once you land on the Lists page, you can add a title in the space where it says Create List and then go on to manage it as for the To-do list.

Deleting or Archiving a List

You might want to delete a list once you've no use for it. The only way to do this is via the App manually (you cannot use you voice). On your mobile device you can swipe left on the title of your list to either Edit the title, or Archive it. Once archived you can tap on View Archive at the bottom of the page and then in the Archive swipe left on your list again to either Restore the list or Delete it completely.

CJ's Tips: When it comes to shopping lists I would say that the major failing is the clunky way that you have to create the dialogue series to add more than one item at a time to your list by voice. For example, I have one of my Echo devices perfectly placed in the kitchen and what I want to do is wander around and say "Alexa, add milk, bread, apples, ham and chicken to my shopping list" but that doesn't work. So it's great when I'm in the kitchen and remember one item I need to add but if I want to make a long list I'm better off adding it manually.

As is the case when learning about any Echo device and Alexa talent, some casual practice should prove fun and entertaining when a dose of patience is included!

7: Never Forget, Always Be On Time — Reminders, Alarms & Timers

For any voice command you read in this chapter be sure to use your wake word ("Alexa", "Amazon", etc) first.

For me, Alexa shines as a personal assistant in these categories. While reminders and alarms are similar, let's look at them separately to learn the nuances of each. Note that in the App menu the page label is just **Reminders & Alarms**, but Timers live here too!

Reminders

This is a quick, easy way to avoid forgetting something urgent or important. A friend of mine stops by to see her elderly father several times a week and sets Reminders for him for the following day or two. When she can't get there in person, she calls her dad and does it remotely with her father's phone on Speaker mode.

Reminders can be set and managed manually or with voice, though using voice is easier.

To set and manage Reminders with voice:

- Say "Remind me to call the mechanic at 1pm"

- If you forget to give a time, Alexa will ask for one, and if you say "1," Alexa will ask, "Is that 1:00 in the morning or afternoon?" or similar.

- If you specify time but not date, Alexa will set up the reminder for today, so be sure to give the day, such as "tomorrow" or "Wednesday" for days this week, or give a date such as October 6.

- To cancel a Reminder, use the day and time rather than what you wanted to be reminded of, so say, "Cancel the reminder for 1pm today," and Alexa will ask for clarification if needed.

- **Note:** You cannot currently edit a Reminder using voice.

To set and manage Reminders manually:

- Go to the **Reminders & Alarms** page where tabs for **Reminders**, **Alarms** and **Timers** appear.

- Select Reminders.

- Select + **Add Reminder**, and a form will appear.

- Fill in the spaces for Remind me to..., Date and Time.

- Select which device you want the reminder to be given on.

- Select **Cancel** or **Save** as appropriate.

- Your reminders appear on the **Reminder** page in chronological order of when they will occur, not when created.

- Manage any Reminder by selecting it, and you'll be taken to a page where you can Edit it or Mark as Completed.

- If you select **Edit**, you'll be taken to a page where you can edit the Reminder by selecting any of the details or **Delete** the Reminder.

- When editing a Reminder using the Alexa App on a computer, you must click away from the detail you edited, so that it is not highlighted, before the Save option becomes active.

Completed Reminders: Select the Completed Reminders tab from below the active list to view them. You're not currently able to delete them from this list. They might jog your memory about whether you did something on the list, though being reminded of it is not a guarantee you followed through. For example, a completed reminder on this list doesn't mean a person remembered to take their medication or feed the dog!

Alarms

Alexa gives you a range of alarm options, which we'll get to shortly, but first, here are the basics. Oddly, you currently cannot set an alarm manually, only using your voice, so let's begin there.

Setting and managing Alarms using voice:

- Say, "Set an alarm for 6am"

- Alexa will display the alarm and say, "Alarm set for 6am"

- Say "Cancel the alarm for 6am," and Alexa will say, "6am alarm canceled"

- If an alarm is on and you request another alarm for 7am, Alexa will say, "Second alarm set for 7am," and both alarms will show on the App

- For repeating alarms, say, "Set an alarm for":
  - 6am every day
  - 2pm every Friday
  - 7:30am on weekends

- If you forget to specify AM or PM, Alexa will ask, "Is that 6 in the morning or the evening?"

- If you don't respond, Alexa will ask again after a few seconds, and if you don't respond to the second query, no alarm will be set.

- All Alarms appear on the main Alarms page with boxes turned On/ Off, indicators shown such as "Every day," with On alarms listed first.

Managing Alarms manually:

- Go to **Reminders & Alarms** and select **Alarms**.

- Use the box next to any alarm to turn it On and Off as desired.

- Select any Alarm to edit it, and a page will display where you can edit the Time, Alarm Sound, choose Repeats options including Never and Delete the alarm if you wish.

- When you've edited the alarm, select **Save Changes** or **Cancel**.

Manage Alarm Volume & Sound manually:

- On the App on your mobile there is a **Settings** link at the bottom of the page for the alarms.

- Change the Alarm, Timer and Notification Volume by dragging the button on the slide bar (Note that this does not change the volume for any other device function, only the volume of the alarm itself).

- Under Custom Sounds, the **Alarm** box will show the Alarm Default Sound, which can be changed by expanding the box using the > shaped caret.

CJ's Tips: If you set up an alarm to go off at the same time every day of the week you won't be able to cancel that alarm for just one day if you don't need it, you have to cancel the whole weekly alarm. Consequently, although it takes me a little longer to set up, I tend to set up an alarm for each day that I need it giving me full control over each alarm.

Also, do check out Celebrity alarm sounds, these change over time and some of them are pretty funny. Failing that, the more traditional alarm sounds are worth exploring to find the one that suits you best; or you can also opt for your favorite song to be the sound that plays for your alarm.

Timers

If you're like me, you may well use Timers for a range of purposes, some which overlap with Reminders. These are simple functions, so this can be quick:

- Timers can be set for 1 second to 24 hours.

- Timers must be set with voice, so say, "Set a timer for 45 minutes" or "Cancel the timer".

- You can name a timer so try saying, "Set pizza timer for 10 mins"

- Multiple timers can be set to run concurrently.

- Active timers will display and count down on the App.

- Note that timers can only be paused manually through the App; do this by tapping on them when they're displayed on a device with a touch screen, such as your tablet or mobile phone.

- Select **Manage timer volume** to be taken to the **Settings** page to adjust Alarm, Timer and Notification Volume.

CJ's Tips: I can't really think of when a timer would be useful in a car setting – perhaps for playing a game of I Spy? But using Alexa on your phone to set multiple named timers are great in the kitchen when you're cooking. Set and name timers for every element of the meal you're making so each timer also becomes a reminder of what's finished cooking or what needs to happen next.

8: Let's See What She Can Do — Alexa Skills

For any voice command you read in this chapter be sure to use your wake word ("Alexa", "Amazon", etc) first.

Alexa Skills are like "apps" for your Alexa-enabled devices. In the same way that you download apps to your tablet or phone for added functionality, you can add (enable) Skills for Alexa that allow you to do more with Alexa. Adding and using these skills is super easy and there are currently more than 70,000 Skills to choose from, and the number grows daily. Skills are loosely grouped into 23 categories currently. Some are good, many are bad, there are sure to be a few of interest for every Echo device owner. For a complete overview of Alexa Skills visit this page of the Amazon website: https://amzn.to/2pN2hC5

Get Familiar with Skills

Once you've enabled Skills you'll be able to use voice control via your Echo Auto to enjoy them – for example you can play the Song Quiz Skill whilst on a long road trip, by saying, "play Song Quiz".

But first you need to enable the Skill and this has to be done manually!

So start your Skills adventure by getting to know what's available. There are three ways to browse Skills, and all begin on the ***Skills & Games*** page on the Alexa App on your mobile. The landing page defaults to a page called ***Discover*** skills that has various rotating and scrollable tabs that link to information about certain Skills or skills categories. Along the top of the landing page you'll also see where to go to search for skills via ***Categories***; and a link to Your Skills, which will be populated once you've enabled some.

8: LET'S SEE WHAT SHE CAN DO — ALEXA SKILLS

CJ's Tips: Actually, this is one area of the Alexa App that I think is easier to deal with on your PC or Mac, since there are so many Skills to consider and having a larger screen to view them on makes it easier. So, on your PC or Mac, you'll see that the default setting on the *Skills* landing page is to show *All Skills*. Near the top right is a tab called *Your Skills*, which will be populated as you enable Skills for your use. Once you are adding Skills, you'll likely toggle back and forth between the All Skills and Your Skills lists quite a bit.

OK, so here's how to find Skills that will enhance your Alexa experience.

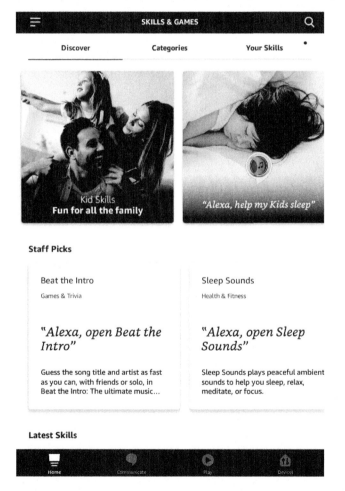

Option 1: Scan *the rows/ tabs* of Skills on the *All Skills* or Discover skills landing page.

61

Option 2: Explore the *Categories* tab where Skills are organized in over 20 categories including:

- Newest Arrivals
- Business & Finance
- Communication
- Connected Car
- Education & Reference
- Food & Drink
- Games & Trivia
- Kids
- Lifestyle
- Movies & TV
- Music & Audio
- News
- Productivity
- Shopping
- Smart Home
- Social
- Sports
- Travel & Transportation
- Weather

Select any category to browse the Skills in it. There will likely be several Skills and you can organize your browsing by choosing the "Sort by" options to the right of the results (Relevance, Customer Rating, Release Date or Featured).

Note that the *Connected Car* category is where you'll find Skills that have been developed by different car and travel companies, such as Garmin, Tesla, Mercedes, Skoda, Honda, Hyundai, CarLock, Evie Assistant, GasBuddy and so on. There are also some fun game skills here specific for car journeys like the Car Color Game – a road trip staple for families across the world! As you're now going to be regularly accessing Alexa in your car via the Echo Auto, it is worth having a good explore here to see if there are any Skills that will enhance your specific driving experience. And do also check out the Travel & Transportation category, which may have additional skills relevant to your journey!

CJ's Tips: These rows are followed by a list of all the Skills in the category. It can be a long list! Currently, there are over 10,000 Skills in the Games & Trivia category, so rather than scrolling through the options, I used the search box to narrow the list to skills related to a personal interest such as word games. 194 results appeared, which was still too many results, so I used the "Sort by" options to narrow the search further.

Option 3: Use the Search box to find a Skill for something very specific (e.g., ecobee, weather Canada, Corvette) or to see if there is one related to one of your interests. For a random sampling, I typed in:

- "Chinese" and received 72 search results related to learning the language or one of the dialects, cuisine, the Chinese calendar and zodiac, etc.

- "Flowers" — 40 results about ordering flowers, facts and trivia, state flowers, etc.

- "Michigan" — 46 results about trivia, history, several state universities, winning lottery numbers, snow reports for skiing, information from news outlets, etc.

Again, the results can be narrowed using the Sort By options at the top right of the results list or by adding a word or two to your search query — "Chinese language", or "University of Michigan", for example. For something like "news" with more than 2500 results, you'll have to search a specific news organization, news about a topic, city, event or similarly narrow term.

Enable Alexa Skills and Use Them

When you're ready to put a Skill into action, the first step is to enable it, which is like turning it on for use with your Alexa account.

It's important to note that some of the Skills require creating and/ or linking to an account or subscription separate from Amazon, so additional steps might be required. Recently, I enabled the Allrecipes Skill and discovered I had to open an account on the Allrecipes site and link to it to get the most from the Skill.

Here's how to enable and use an Alexa Skill:

- Use one of the options above to locate a skill you want to enable, and select the skill. You can also browse and Enable Skills on Amazon. com

- Select **Enable Skill**, and after a few seconds, the box will switch to Disable Skill, which means it's been enabled and will appear in the **Your Skills** list.

- Note that you might be required to link the Skill to your Amazon account, in which case follow the prompts to do so – this will usually require you to log into your Amazon account.

- Alternately, some Skills can be enabled by voice, for example say, "Enable the Rainforest Sounds Skill".

- To use any Enabled Skill, include the name of the Skill when making a request such as "Alexa, play rainforest sounds".

- **Note:** Skills in use do not appear on the **Now Playing** page or **Player**, so to control them, say "Stop," "Pause," "Resume" or similar.

Get the Most from the Skills You Enable

The more familiar you are with the Skill's capabilities, the more it will benefit you. Here are suggestions for optimizing a Skill's usefulness:

- If another action is offered along with Enabling the Skill, such as Manage in News Briefing (common for Skills from news organizations, and covered later), select the option to learn about it and decide whether to use the feature.

- Read the ***About the Skill*** section to acquaint yourself with its capabilities.

- Review the ***Try Saying*** suggestions to get the Skill to do what you want and additional suggestions in the About information.

- Learn the ***Invocation Name*** for the Skill (found under Skill Details) to be sure Alexa will put it to work when you want to use it.

- Browse the ***Customers Have Also Enabled*** section for similar or complementary ideas.

- Read reviews, and, if interested, add a review after you've used the Skill for a few weeks.

- Select ***Having Trouble with This Skill*** to get help using it from the source of the Skill.

Disable an Alexa Skill

Over time, the Your Skills section can become crowded with Skills you don't use. They're easy to remove.

- Select the Skill from Your Skills list.

- Select Disable Skill, and the box will flip to Enable Skill to indicate it isn't enabled and the Skill will disappear from your list.

CJ's Tips: Whilst researching this book I've explored more than 800 Skills and Enabled more than 500, but my Skills list currently has 48 Skills; I use some daily and others only occasionally.

The Skills I rely on the most are those that save me time, are easy to use and/or offer genuine value. If they're a hassle, a time-waster or not the easiest or best way to do things, I either disable them immediately or as soon as the novelty wears off or when I occasionally go through the list to get rid of unused Skills. Some have features that are easy to use and features that are a hassle.

You'll soon see that there are sometimes several Skills for some purposes.

Searching Skills for "find my phone" yielded seven results, "restaurant finder" showed ten options and "control lights" produced a list of 48 smart home Skills. And in the case of Smart Home Skills, some require a specific brand of home automation equipment. Look for your brand's logo in the results list. If you don't find it, explore some of the top-rated Skills by reading the About information, Requirements for its use and Reviews. Reading the information is a good approach when choosing any Skill from a results list.

When I'm undecided about which of two or three Skills to choose, I enable both or all and use them alternately. I often use one right after another, and do that every day for a week or so. This is a better way to determine which Skill is right for me than to try one for a week and then try another. I like an immediate, one-after-the-other comparison.

The point I'm delicately trying to make is that there are many Skills that...just aren't very good. It's worth putting in some time to find the gems that you'll use over and over, but be prepared to wade through quite a lot of rubbish!

Alexa Skills Blueprint

This is a very recent development at Amazon, and one that I'm looking forward to exploring further. Basically, the idea of Skills Blueprint is that you can use pre-loaded, customizable templates provided by Amazon to create your own unique Skill.

For example, you could create a trivia game skill about your family history to play on a road trip; or you could build your own story – including sound effects – where you and/or your kids are the heroes!

If this is something that appeals to you, go straight to the Amazon Skill Blueprint site at blueprints.amazon.com; click on the template that interests you and follow the instructions to create your very own Skill which is then be associated with the Alexa-enabled devices that are linked to your Amazon account. Simple!

9: 21ˢᵗ Century Living — Smart Home

For any voice command you read in this chapter be sure to use your wake word ("Alexa", "Amazon", etc) first.

A really neat way you can use your Echo Auto is to control Smart Home equipment whilst en route home – for example asking Alexa to "turn on porch lights", or "set thermostat in the living room to 76 degrees".

Of course, this will only be relevant if you have that Smart Home technology in your home already and if that equipment is already integrated with Alexa.

If you're already integrating smart technology into your home, then learning to control it with Alexa's help will be one of the easier parts of the curve. There's a four-step process that is straightforward and usually successful. If you're new to smart home devices then I recommend you visit the Amazon Smart Home page to familiarize yourself with the possible options.

Note that the initial set up – where you're linking your smart home devices to Alexa – needs to be done at home, manually, with the devices close to hand. If your smart home device is compatible with Alexa, it will have its own Skill. Smart home tasks are considered Skills and used as such. You'll be well prepared for the information here if you've read the previous chapter and enabled a few Skills.

Here are the steps. Each is explained in detail below:

1. Prepare your smart home device for linking.

2. Enable the Skill associated with the smart home device.

3. Ask Alexa to discover the device to connect the two and to use Alexa

to control the smart home device.

4. Use the Alexa App to organize your smart home devices for optimal use.

Amazon suggests we cover a few common-sense security tips for using smart home devices with Alexa, so let's do that first:

- Follow the device's instructions for safe, recommended uses.

- Confirm that requests have been carried out — especially tasks related to your home's safety and security (security system, exterior lighting, door locks, garage door, HVAC, appliances, and similar).

- Turn off the microphones on Alexa-enabled devices if you do not want Alexa to respond to voice commands when safety and security cannot be ensured (such as when adults are away from home).

- Remember that once a device is connected, anyone can use Alexa to control it, so make sure those in your household and guests understand safe operation of smart home devices.

Okay, let's get rolling.

Step 1: Prepare your Smart Home Device

This step ensures your device is compatible and optimized for use with Alexa:

- Verify that your smart home device is compatible with Amazon Alexa, which can be done by searching for it on the Skills page of the Alexa App or Amazon.com, checking the packaging, contacting the manufacturer or viewing its website and looking for the device on the Alexa smart home shopping page that includes all compatible devices.

- Download the manufacturer's app for the smart home device to any mobile device (preferably the same one that you're using to manage the Alexa App).

- Use the manufacturer's app to set up the smart home device/ equipment on the same Wi-Fi network your mobile phone is on.

- Download and install the latest software updates for the smart home device.

Step 2: Enable the Device's Skill

Go to the smart home Devices page in the Alexa App. Note that on the App via your mobile phone you need to tap on the icon depicting a house with two switches inside which takes you to a landing page for all your smart home **Devices**. You cannot get to this page via the Menu on the mobile version of the Alexa App.

- At the top of the **Devices** landing page you'll see a + plus sign, tap on that and choose **Add Device** form the options. Then scroll down to find the device you want to link.

- Choose the brand and type of your smart home device, if asked. The App will remind you to download the smart home device's app (which you should already have done) and then press **Continue**.

- The **Continue** button will take you directly to the Skills page for your smart home device, which you can then **Enable**. Alternately, Skills can be searched on Amazon.com (https://amzn.to/2ONKNni).

- Note that, before you **Enable** the Skills, you may want to check out the details of how the device works familiarize yourself with its capabilities, by tapping on the See More link in the Skills details.

- Select the **Enable** button, and when it changes to **Disable**, you'll know the Skill is enabled.

- If prompted, sign into the smart home device account to link it to your Alexa account.

- Follow any further prompts given to complete setting up the smart home device on Alexa.

Note: A list of your Enabled smart home devices will populate on the **Devices > All Devices** page in your Alexa App. Select any of the Skills to Disable it or to learn more about it.

Step 3: Ask Alexa to Discover the Device

This can be done two ways:

- Say, "Discover devices".

- Go to the **Smart Home** page on the App on your PC, select **Devices**, and then select the Discover tab.

Step 4: Set Up Groups, Scenes and Routines

As you connect smart home devices to Alexa, you can then set them up to work together by putting them into groups, scenes or routines. Now let's look at the first two options, we'll come back to the Routines later.

It may seem at first that there is no real difference between the Group option and the Scenes option; but in fact they have different functions.

Basically, when your smart home devices are put together in a Group the command you can give them via Alexa is simply to turn those devices on or off simultaneously, so for example turning on three specific light bulbs in the bedroom at the same time.

However, the Scenes option allows you to predetermine the state of those devices, for example if you want the light bulbs to be on low and the thermostat to go down to a lower temperature at bedtime (in this case the Scene would be named Bedtime and the command to Alexa would be "Alexa, turn on Bedtime").

The other big difference is that you set up a Group within the Alexa App; whereas to set up Scenes you need to first configure those scenes in the smart home device's app, and then those specific device scenes will be listed in the Scenes page on the Alexa App, where you can then control those scenes via Alexa.

Effectively the Scenes page simply shows you the different scenes you have already set up and then allows you to manage them with Alexa voice commands.

How to Set Up Groups:

On the **Devices** landing page tap on **+ sign** (top right hand corner) and then **Add Group**:

- Choose a name for the group from the options provided, or add your own name and tap **Next**. Remember that Alexa won't comprehend words with numbers or symbols in them like kitch3n lights or #kitchen lights@.

- Add the smart home devices that you want to be part of that group (remember this means that these devices that will work together with a single command.)

- Try the Group by making a request of Alexa appropriate to the Group's functionality ("Turn on Kitchen," or "Turn off Downstairs" for example).

- To edit or delete the Group, go to the Devices landing page, and you'll see the Groups you've create. Select the Group > Edit and then you can delete by tapping on the trashcan icon, or edit the group accordingly.

CJ's Tips: Alexa uses voice recognition to understand what you say and connect it with digital content such as the name of a group you type into the App. For this reason, give groups names that won't confuse Alexa. To be on the safe side, I recommend sticking with the Common Group names that Alexa offers.

How to Manage Scenes:

First configure specific Scenes within the smart home device's app. For example, if you want to create a scene with the Philips Hue smart light, then you need to go into the Hue app to set up that scene.

- Give the same Scene name to all the devices you want to be in that Scene (for example if you want the lights off and the thermostat to go down at bedtime, then name the Scene for both devices "Bedtime").

- All Scenes that you have set up on your smart home devices should appear in the detail of the devices you see in the **All Devices** page

- You can now use voice command to activate those Scenes, using the name you've set for that Scene ("turn on Bedtime" for example).

Setting Up Routines:

So here's the idea of Routines. We all have daily habits and routines, from getting up and dressed in the morning to coming home from work and cooking dinner in the evening. Now you can group certain Alexa smart home and Skills features together to compliment those daily routines and have them all start/activate at the same time, either with one single voice command or at a set time each day.

The difference of Routines compared to Groups and Scenes is this: Groups simply allow you to link smart home devices together to turn on and off; Scenes allow you to set up only smart home devices to work together at certain levels according to the scene parameters you've set; whilst Routines allow you to link smart home devices and certain Alexa Skills to run anytime you give the voice command for that routine.

For example, if you wake up at the same time each day you can program a morning routine for Alexa to turn up your thermostat, turn on your Smart Home kettle, give you the weather forecast and catch you up on news headlines via your Flash Briefing. Either set this routine to start at 6.30 am every morning or start the routine by saying something like "Alexa, start the day" or "Alexa, good morning" or whatever you like!

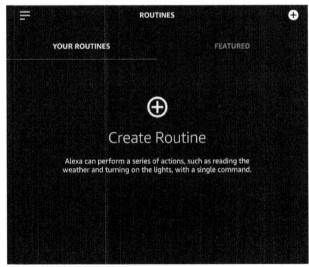

So, to set up a Routine, here's what to do:

- In the Alexa App go to *Menu > Routines*. You will see that Alexa has some suggested Featured routines. For now, ignore this and tap the big + *Create Routine* in the middle the page, of the + *sign* at the top right of the page.

- Now you will have the options to *When this happens* and *Add action*.

- Tap the + *sign* next to *When this happens* and chose and option, the obvious being either to create a voice command for your routine (example, "Alexa, good morning") or schedule a set time for your routine. When scheduling a time, you not only set the time of day but can also choose to have the routine happen on a specific day, every day, week days or weekends. You can also link your routine to a certain smart home device activating, or the pressing of an Echo Button, or for when you dismiss a particular alarm.

- Follow the prompts to save what cue or condition is used to activate the routine. Don't forget to press Save when you're done.

- Now tap the + *sign* next to *Add action*. You will now be able to choose from the options I mentioned earlier, *Music, News, Smart Home, Traffic, Weather* or *Alexa Says* (this last option is quite fun – offering a number of stock phrases that Alexa can use to reply to your Routine opener). There is also an option to set the volume for your Routine feature marked Audio Control. Setting up some of these features is discussed in the relevant chapters of this guide.

- For now, tap *Add* to include one or all of these features to your new Routine and then tap *Create*.

- You may also be prompted to choose which Alexa enabled device plays the routine, if you have more than one Alexa-enabled device for example. Again, don't forget the tap on *Save* when you've got everything set up how you want.

Your new routine will now appear in your list of routines and you can tap again on any routine to edit it, temporarily toggle the routine on or off, and delete the routine if you wish.

Troubleshooting Alexa and Smart Home Device Set Up

If Alexa doesn't discover your smart home device, try these tips in this order. They will troubleshoot and solve most issues.

Device Issues: Double-check that:

- Your smart home device is compatible with Alexa.

- That you have Enabled the device's Skill.

- That you have downloaded the device's app.

- That you have downloaded the latest software updates for the device.

- For a Philips Hue Bridge, be sure to press the button on the Bridge before trying to discover devices.

- Disable and Enable the smart home device.

- In the Alexa App, choose the Forget option for the smart home device to unlink it from Alexa, and then try to reconnect it.

Wi-Fi Issues: The device that you access Alexa from and your smart home devices must be on the same Wi-Fi network. Personal networks are best; school and work networks you don't control might not allow unrecognized devices to connect.

Note: Some smart home devices can only connect to the 2.4 GHz Wi-Fi band. If you have a dual-band network, make sure it is set to the 2.4 GHz band.

Discover your smart home devices again: If you've made any changes discussed here, including the Wi-Fi network or band or a group name say, "Discover devices." Alexa will let you know if they are found or will say "I didn't find any devices." If this occurs, contact the smart home device manufacturer for further assistance, since it is up to the device manufacturer, not Amazon, to ensure that their devices are compatible with Alexa devices.

10: Your Highly Capable Personal Assistant — Things to try

For any voice command you read in this chapter be sure to use your wake word ("Alexa", "Amazon", etc) first.

This is a large section of the Alexa App and could be a book of its own!

The good news is that many of the ***Things to Try*** have been discussed in other sections, and the ones I don't talk about anywhere are very straightforward and easy to use with the few words of explanation given in the Alexa App. Our purpose in this chapter is to shed light on Things to Try that haven't been mentioned but require some explanation.

CJ's Tips: Note that some of these features need to be set up manually first, so it's best to explore the ***Things to Try*** pages from the safety and comfort of your own home before heading out in the car.

To get started, select the ***Things to Try*** from the menu in the Alexa App to explore them for yourself or to follow along with this discussion. The Things to Try section is just a list. When you select any of them, you will usually be taken to the ***Help & Feedback*** section for an explanation. The list serves as an easy place to find topics you want more information about.

Here are some of the useful and interesting ***Things to Try*** that haven't been detailed already in the book:

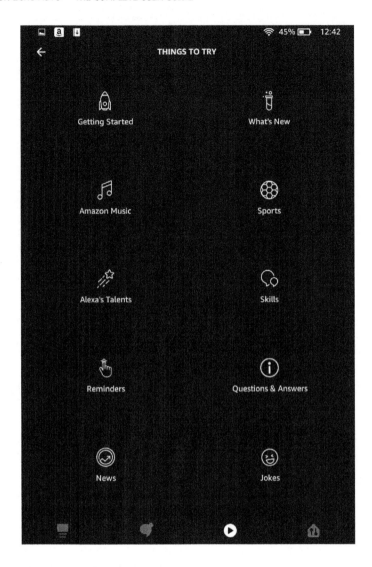

What's new?

I like to keep up with Alexa's capabilities, so I check this section weekly, at least. There's always something new. It's a mixed and disorganized bag ranging from simple, fun stuff ("Drum roll") to interesting information (the ability to give publication dates and authors for popular books) to new Skills ("Give me a quote") to new Alexa-enabled devices (this week, TV remotes from Sony, Logitech and Broadlink). It's a potpourri of fresh possibilities with Alexa.

Ask Questions

If you can think it, the question might be worth asking. I ask these types of questions quite often:

- What time it is here or elsewhere?
- Conversions of weight, measurements temperature, money.
- Spellings/synonyms/definitions.
- People and place facts.
- Math.

Check and Manage Your Calendar

Alexa can link to calendars from Google, Apple and Microsoft.

- Go to **Settings**, and scroll down to the **Accounts** section to **Calendar**.
- Choose the calendar you want to connect, and select Link _____ account.
- Link another calendar, if desired.
- Say, "What's on my calendar?" "What's my next appointment?" or similar.
- Say, "Add a 9:30am meeting to my calendar".

Discover New Alexa Skills

See the Skills Chapter for a more in-depth look at Skills, but if you want to hear about the latest releases:

- Say, "What are popular Skills?"
- Say, "What new Skills do you have?"
- Browse the Skills store mentioned earlier where every Skill can be found and Enabled.

Find Local Businesses and Restaurants

If you haven't set your location yet, this is a good time to do that, so Alexa knows where to search. In the Alexa App manually select **Menu > Settings > Device settings**. Then choose your device (your phone) and scroll down to **Device location**. Select that option and you can enter or change your address there. Don't forget to tap **Save** when you're done. The more information you provide, the more accurate Alexa can be in telling you how far you are from businesses and restaurants.

Now you can ask Alexa to help you find local businesses. Here are things to try:

- "Find a Mexican restaurant".

- "Is the post office open?"

- "What clothing stores are nearby?"

- "What supermarkets are near me?"

- "What is the phone number for B&V Asian Market?"

Your search doesn't have to be local either. When planning a trip, you can ask Alex to find any of these things in another town.

- "Is there a shoe store in Grand Rapids?"

- "Pharmacy in Plano, Texas".

- "Is there Crossfit in Raleigh, North Carolina?"

As well as Alexa reporting the result of your search to you, all searches produce Cards, so you'll have the results right in front of you on the Alexa App with detailed information including, where applicable Yelp ratings.

Search results might be varied, especially when there are only a few good options. When using Alexa in a rural area, I requested a "sporting goods store," and got one accurate result and four others, ranging from a used firearms dealer to a marina. See how you do with your searches!

CJ's Tips: Alexa is far from perfect yet, but I'm often impressed with the information I can get from her. If I need to call a local shop or business I always ask Alexa for the number first before reaching for the phone book or doing a search online; more often than not, I get the info I'm looking for.

Find Traffic Information

Alexa can give you an estimated time for your commute and the fastest route.

- In **Settings** on the Alexa App, manually scroll down and select **Traffic**.
- Add or change your current address, your "From,".
- Add a destination, your "To".
- Stops along the way can be added too.
- Later, select **Change address** to edit any of the locations.

Once set, you can then ask Alexa, "What's my traffic?" While I use this for the drive I make most often, it can be convenient for determining the time for other driving routes by changing the "From," "To" or both.

Get Weather Forecasts

Once Alexa knows your location in **Settings > Your Device > Location**, you can hear local weather information and also view the forecast on the Card produced. Ask about weather in other cities around the globe too. Common questions Alexa can answer include:

- "What's the weather?"
- "Show me the forecast".
- "Will it rain tomorrow?"
- "How warm will it be today?"

There are many ways to answer the question, but Alexa replies to all of them with the same information — verbally sharing current and expected weather conditions for the next 24 hours and showing an extended forecast within the App.

Go to the Movies

This section uses your location to access local movie schedules and can give you information for movie schedules in cities you'll be visiting. I get the best results with questions like these:

- "What movies are playing?"

- "What movies are playing at [name of theater complex]?"

- "When will Indiana Jones play tomorrow?"

- "Show me the trailer for the movie Dunkirk".

- "Tell me about the Aquaman movie".

Hear the News

Alexa offers something called a **Flash Briefing**. Many news and entertainment organizations including NPR, NBC, FOX, BBC and ESPN make brief overviews of the news, such as you might hear at the top or bottom of the hour, and those summaries can be added to your Flash Briefing.

To select which summaries you want to hear in your Briefing, and to start and manage it:

- Manually go to **Settings > Alexa Preferences > Flash Briefing** to toggle On or Off the default options, if there are any.

- Go to Skills and search your favorite news, sports, weather and entertainment stations (there are new media coming onboard every week), and enable the Skill.

- If it offers a Briefing summary, that will show in your list of Flash Briefing choices in Settings.

- Toggle On or Off the briefings, and you can make changes when desired.

- Ask "What's the news," "Give me my flash briefing," "Flash briefing," "What's in the news?" or something similar, and you'll hear the entire briefing, one organization at a time.

- Note that the briefing does not show on the Now Playing page or the Player.

CJ's Tips: Once you've toggled the briefings ON, a blue Edit Order options will appear at the top of the page. Click on this and then tap/ click and drag each of your news sources into your preferred order of importance. I find that there are a couple of news sources I value above the others, so I definitely want to hear them first. Don't forget to tap/ click Done when you're finished to preserve the order you've chosen.

Get Your Sports Updates

Give Alexa a team name and say, "score," and you'll hear the score of the most recent game. If you want to hear the latest scores and the next game for all the teams you follow, go manually to **Settings > Sports** to search and select those teams. Then, you'll get the answer when you ask questions like:

- "Sports scores".

- "When do the Seattle Mariners play next?"

- "NBA scores".

- "Score for Real Madrid".

- "How many touchdowns did Odell Beckham junior score?"

- "How many homeruns does Aaron Judge have?"

Many major colleges can be followed too in football and basketball. The leagues currently supported on the Alexa App are:

North American Leagues:

- MLB — Major League Baseball

- MLS — Major League Soccer

- NBA — National Basketball Association

- NCAA — National Collegiate Athletic Association

- NFL — National Football League

- NHL — National Hockey League

- WNBA — Women's National Basketball Association

European Leagues:

English Premier League

FA Cup — Football Association Challenge Cup

German Bundesliga

UEFA Champions League

CJ's Tips: Above is a list of all the teams officially supported via Alexa, but I've found that I can get information for many other teams just by searching for them in the search box at *Settings* > *Sports Update* within the Alexa App.

Calling and Messaging

Important: You should note that Alexa calling and messaging services on your Echo Auto will use data, minutes and/ or texts from your smartphone plan.

This Alexa feature has tremendous potential and will become more useful as the universe of Alexa users expands. If you know three or more people with Alexa devices, this section might be worth reading now. Otherwise, it's here when Alexa catches on more broadly among your friends, family members and business contacts. You can communicate with other Alexa users if you have both downloaded the Alexa App (note that you don't necessarily need to have a specific Amazon Echo device to download the Alexa App onto your phone), and inputted the contact's information correctly.

Setting up Calling and Messaging

- Ensure you have downloaded onto your phone the latest Alexa App for iOS 9.0 or higher (https://apple.co/2xhWycQ) or for Android 5.0 or higher (https://bit.ly/2fBWcUi)

- Manually select the Conversations icon (the speech bubble) at the bottom of the page, and follow the instructions to sign up for Alexa Calling and Messaging and to verify your mobile number.

- Import your contacts, and those who have also signed up for Calling and Messaging will appear in your Contacts list.

- To add or edit contacts for this service, update your phone's local Address book and then open the Alexa App.

- Give your contacts names you'll remember, now simply ask Alexa to call one of them, and Alexa will dial the number associated with that name.

- Calling and Messaging can be used on Echo Auto, Echo, Echo Show, Echo Dot and Fire Tablet with Alexa, or between non-Echo users that have the Alexa App on their phone.

- Note that some devices with a screen also offer a video calling option.

- If you ever wish to deregister from Calling and Messaging, contact Amazon customer service at 1.877.375.9365.

Calls

- Tell your Alexa-using friends and family about Calling and Messaging, and encourage them to get set up.

- To make a call from your Echo Auto say, "Call Aunt Ellen," and Alexa will begin the call.

- When someone is calling you, Alexa will let you know who is calling.

- To answer a call, say, "Answer" or select the Answer button on the devices screen, if applicable.

- To ignore the call, say, "Ignore the call."

- To end a call, say, "Hang up".

There's a video about calling with Alexa here: https://amzn.to/2AOKbbf

Messages

- Messages are recorded and played back to the recipient rather than transcribed and read by Alexa.

- To send a message from the Echo Auto, say, "Send a message to Sara Smith," and Alexa will prompt you for the message and send your message when you complete it.

- To hear messages on the Echo Auto, say, "Play my messages".

- When more than one phone number is synced with Alexa, you can name the numbers and say, "Play messages for _____" to hear only your messages.

There's a video about messaging with Alexa here: https://amzn.to/2vqMD2n

Drop in

- Drop in is typically set up among two or more Echo devices in a single household, between family members and BFFs.

- Drop in means that people in separate parts of the home, or in different homes, or from the car can communicate immediately without making a formal call.

- Drop in must be enabled in the mobile Alexa App for all devices that will use the capability.

- In the Conversations section of the mobile App, select a contact and turn On the Drop in button if they have drop-in privileges with you.

- To drop in on one of your own devices, say something like, "Drop in on my living room Echo".

- The names of the devices in your home can be changed in the

Settings on the Alexa App.

- Friends and family with Alexa can also drop in on each other, but you must both first enable Drop In with your Contacts list. Go to the Contacts section of the App, select a contact and turn on the Drop-in button if you want them to have drop-in privileges with you. Note that, on the Conversations landing page of the Alexa App on your mobile you can also see your Contacts by tapping the icon of a person on the top right corner of the page.

There's a video with complete Drop in details here: amzn. to/2yCLRjR

Announcements

A relatively new addition to the options for Calling and Messaging, the Announcements option works like a one-way intercom where you can basically announce a short message, such as "Dinner's ready!" or "I'm one my way home" to other Alexa-enabled devices on your account. For example, from your Echo Show that's in your kitchen to the Echo Dot that's in your kid's room and the Echo that's in the home office. Or from your Echo Auto (via the Alexa App on your mobile phone) back to your Echo devices at home.

This is basically similar to Drop In, but just for short voice-only messages. Or you could think of it as a voice version of a text message! Here's how to do it:

- You can use your voice to make any announcement, say "Announce (I'm on my way home!)" and your other Alexa-enabled devices will chime and play the announcement.

- Note that mobile devices with the Alexa App (i.e. your mobile phone) and Echo Auto can send but not receive announcements.

While I've covered the essential details, there is a section on Alexa Calling and Messaging FAQs located here: www.amzn.to/2xy8nJ1

Kids Skills & Safety

On the **Things to Try** page you'll also see a link to Kids Skills; this provides an easy link up to all the Skills that have been designed with children in mind, such as story and joke telling, games and quizzes.

Access to Kids Skills are turned off by default, so to access them via your Echo Auto then you'll first need to manually **Enable Kids Skills**. Once enabled you can then **Explore Kids Skills**, and then set up each Skill you like use.

Note that when you enable access to Kids Skills you are automatically allowing Amazon to store data from the Skill when it is used including voice-recordings. As with other voice interactions with Alexa, you can delete them by going to **Settings > History**.

Other things to consider concerning the safe use of your Echo Auto when children are present, is to turn off **Voice Purchasing** in your shopping preferences and to turn on **Explicit Filter** in your music preferences! Both of these options can be found and managed in the **Settings**.

11: Your Perfect Fit
— Alexa Settings

For any voice command you read in this chapter be sure to use your wake word ("Alexa", "Amazon", etc) first.

The Settings section is where you manually control how the Alexa App functions to suit your style. So, let's walk through the Settings to get familiar with their contents and how you can tailor them to suit you. Select **Settings** on the App Menu to be taken to the **Settings Main Page** where we'll get started. Scrolling down the Settings landing page these are the options you'll see:

Your Profile: This is a small section where you can:

- Edit your personal details

- Add your Voice Profile (if you want)

- Ensure your correct mobile number is association with the account.

Account Settings: This section also links to the page where you can set Voice Profiles, but also:

- Enable **Voice Purchasing**

- Create your **Amazon Household**

- Find the very important **History** section and **Delete the Voice Recordings** that Alexa keeps from the voice requests you've made

.....

CJs Tips: A new function also accessed here, you can now enable Alexa to delete recordings when you say, "delete what I just said" or "delete everything I said today".

.....

87

Device Settings/ Alexa on this Phone: If you tap on ***Device Settings*** the first thing you'll see is a list of the Alexa-enabled devices that you own and linked to your Alexa account. The word "Online" appears beneath any device when it is connected to a Wi-Fi network. Select ***Alexa on this Phone*** from the list for:

- Basic setup, organization and information

- Set and manage your ***Device Location***

- Change Time Zone and ***Measurement Units***

Note that if you have other Echo devices, when you go into the specific device settings for that device you'll see other setting options that are relevant to that device and which are not currently relevant to the Alexa App on your phone, such as Pairing Bluetooth and changing the Wake Word.

Notifications: This section allows you to enable notifications for features such as ***Reminders, Shopping*** and new ***Things to Try***.

Your Locations: Here you can add different addresses (like home or work) and Alexa can use them in reference to reminders and so on. For example, "remind me to call the doctor when I get home".

Privacy: This is a large section of information concerning privacy questions and ***Permissions Management*** for Skills. I recommend you have a good explore here to find out more.

Music: This section lists the music streaming services you've linked to Alexa, along with the user ID for the account, and those available to use with Alexa that don't require an account. Here you can:

- Add and manage music service

- Select the ***Choose Default Music Service*** option to choose a default music library and music station

- Find the ***Profanity Filter***

Flash Briefing: Most news services create short news summaries hourly or several times per day, in many cases to play on radio. Many of those summaries are available for playing on you Echo Auto whenever you want to hear them. Most are Skills, and we've discussed Skills at length. Together, those summaries you choose make your Flash Briefing. To create yours:

- Select **Add Content**

- Browse the list, and select the ones you want. Enable the Skill if necessary.

- Those you choose will be listed here. Toggle on those you want to play.

- Choose **Edit Order** to rearrange the order they are played.

- Say, "Play my Flash Briefing," "What's in the news" or similar, and Alexa will deliver it.

- Say, "Skip" or "Next," and Alexa will move on to the next service in the briefing. I have 11 services in my briefing, but I often hear the top story from a service and then skip to the next or skip the service altogether.

Traffic: This feature was covered in **Things to Try chapter**; your Traffic feature gives you commute times. Input a "From" location, "To" location and stops in between, if desired. Edit them to change your route, and then ask, "What's my commute?"

Sports Update: This feature was also covered in the **Things to Try chapter,** but here's a summary. The feature allows you to follow professional teams and leagues from North America and Europe plus the football and basketball teams for most major colleges in the US. Simply search and choose the teams you want to follow. Then say, "Sports update" to hear latest scores and upcoming games for the teams in your list that are currently in season.

Calendars: Alexa can link to calendars from Google, Microsoft and Apple iCloud. Link your calendars, and add items to them with basic requests such as, "Add appointment at 3pm Thursday to my calendar" and hundreds of similar things. See Check and Manage your Calendar in this guide's **Things to Try chapter.**

Lists: Alexa manages a Shopping List and To-do List for you in the App, and you can create your own lists too. But here is where you need to go if you want to link Alexa to several 3rd party list apps such as *AnyList* and *TodoList*. If you already have an account with one of those services, connecting it with Alexa might make sense. If you don't, it's redundant if you have the ability to make lists in the Alexa App on your phone.

12: Ressources Galore — Help & Feedback

For any voice command you read in this chapter be sure to use your wake word ("Alexa", "Amazon", etc) first.

This section of the Alexa App provides a wealth of information, though we've already covered much of it and referred to it frequently. When selecting an item from Things to Try, for example, you are usually taken here for the explanation. There are things worth mentioning about this section that haven't been covered yet in this guide.

When you click or tap on **Help & Feedback**, at the top you will see the options **Alexa Features**, **Alexa Devices** and **Alexa Companion Devices**. Here's what each option will give you:

Alexa Features – General Alexa User Guide

As you will have guessed, **Alexa Devices** and **Alexa Companion Devices** options will give you information that is particular to your specific device (more about this later).

However, clicking or tapping on **Alexa Features** will produce another page with further sections to explore about the Alexa App that are common to all Alexa-enabled devices, including these worth looking at in more detail:

Alexa Smart Home: This is where you'll get further answers for setting up, controlling and managing your smart home devices, including a useful section for troubleshooting the most common problems.

Music with Alexa, Video with Alexa: Lots of helpful tips to do with playing Music, Video via Alexa, and setting things like playing music on several Echo devices.

Alexa Calling and Messaging: Here is your resource for Calling, Messaging, Drop-In capabilities. The information in this section and its links are comprehensive. You'll find step-by-step instructions to follow for setup and use, if what we discussed earlier isn't clear

This is also where you'll find answers to questions concerning most productivity tasks such as setting alarms, timers, shopping, making lists, getting your traffic, flash briefing and calendar updates and so on.

Alexa Devices - Echo User Guides

To get specific information about the features of specific Echo Devices, you will need to return to the *Help & Feedback* homepage first then go to *Alexa Devices* where you'll find help and tips to manage features specific Echo devices, including for example those that are specific to Echo Devices with a Screen, as managing accessibility features for users with vision or hearing impairments.

Alexa Companion Devices

This section of *Help & Feedback* is for setting up/troubleshooting companion devices such as the Echo Sub, the Echo Link Amp, the Alexa Voice Remote or using Alexa on non-Echo devices such as the Fire TV.

Contact Us

I've had no issues with Alexa that I couldn't solve using the abundance of information found in the Alexa App and on Amazon.com. Because of the good fortune I've had with Alexa, I haven't emailed or called Customer Service. However, if you have problems and can't find answers, don't hesitate to contact Amazon. Feedback is another issue. I have used the Send Feedback option seven times to date to give Amazon my thoughts on how to improve Alexa performance. I bring this up to say that Amazon has always been responsive, so if you contact the company with issues, you can expect that a customer service representative will be in touch.

Legal

If you have questions about how Amazon will use your information or what legal parameters there are for using Alexa, scanning the Legal & Compliance section will provide you with answer

13: Going to the Source — Amazon Pages to Be Familiar With

My goal is to provide you with clear, concise information from the perspective of someone that uses Echo devices and Alexa every day, insight I don't often find when reading pages on Amazon. That's why I wrote this book. Still, there are pages on the website that might help you get the most from your Echo Auto.

Alexa Help: This is a home page with links to information on the broad categories of things Alexa can provide — Music & Entertainment, News & Information, Questions & Answers and everything else covered in this book. http://amzn.to/2k5tsrI

Echo Auto Help: This page, and its many links, overlaps with the Alexa Help page, but the emphasis is just on the Echo Auto.

https://amzn.to/34uWK5q

Echo Auto Help Videos: This page provides general overview videos for many key setup and use tasks. https://amzn.to/2NjI9E9

Before You Go

So there you have it! I trust by now you have your Echo Auto up and running and have become familiar with many of its features. Please drop me a line at cjandersentech@gmail.com if you require any further clarification.

And finally, positive reviews on Amazon.com make a huge difference to the success of independent authors, such as myself. If you found this guide helpful, I would be very grateful if you took a moment to leave a comment. Thank you.

Printed in Great Britain
by Amazon